Metaphors of Identity

The Treatment of Childhood in Selected Québécois Novels

Roseanna Lewis Dufault

Rutherford • Madison • Teaneck
Fairleigh Dickinson University Press
London and Toronto: Associated University Presses

Associated University Presses
440 Forsgate Drive
Cranbury, NJ 08512

Associated University Presses
25 Sicilian Avenue
London WC1A 2QH, England

Associated University Presses
P.O. Box 39, Clarkson Pstl. Stn.
Mississauga, Ontario,
L5J 3X9 Canada

The paper used in this publication meets the requirements of the American National Standard for Permanence of Paper for Printed Library Materials Z39.48-1984.

Library of Congress Cataloging-in-Publication Data

Dufault, Roseanna Lewis, 1954–
  Metaphors of identity : the treatment of childhood in selected Québécois novels / Roseanna Lewis Dufault.
    p. cm.
  Includes bibliographical references (p.) and index.
  ISBN 0-8386-3424-9 (alk. paper)
    1. French-Canadian fiction—Québec (Province)—History and criticism. 2. Identity (Psychology) in literature. 3. Québec (Province) in literature. 4. Children in literature. I. Title.
PQ3912.D83 1991
843—dc20   90-55832
                                                                    CIP

To Cathy and Ray

Contents

Acknowledgments

I would like to thank R. J. S. and K. A. W. for encouragement and support.

A research grant from the Québec Government helped to make this work possible.

Metaphors of Identity

1

Introduction

It has been observed and generally accepted that childhood persists as one of the most enduring themes and leitmotivs of Québécois literature. Images of childhood pervade the works of four of Québec's major poets, Emile Nelligan, Saint-Denys-Garneau, Gatien Lapointe, and Anne Hébert, as Lucille Roy-Hewitson has demonstrated. She affirms that, "pendant plus d'un demi-siècle, le thème de l'enfance semble avoir hanté l'imaginaire québécois" (1980, 35). Including Alain Grandbois in a similar study of Québécois poets, Pierre Chatillon confirms that allusions to childhood recur "avec une continuité, une persistence qu'on peut à bon droit qualifier d'obsessionnelle" (1961, 2).

In a sociological survey of Québécois novels published between 1837 and 1962, Denise Lemieux discovered significant references to childhood in more than two hundred works (1984, 10).

During the 1960s, Marie-Claire Blais observed and criticized Québécois society most effectively from the perspective of her child protagonists, notably Jean-le-Maigre in *Une Saison dans la vie d'Emmanuel* and Pauline Archange in *Manuscrits de Pauline Archange*. Several important writers have produced fictionalized accounts of their own childhood experiences. Claire Martin's *Dans un gant de fer* evokes painful memories of violence and oppression, while Gabrielle Roy's *Rue Deschambault,* Roch Carrier's *Les Enfants du bonhomme dans la lune,* and Joseph Rudel-Tessier's *Roquelune* express a gentler, bittersweet nostalgia for the past. Many prominent

Québécois novelists continue to explore various aspects of this perennial theme. Childhood plays a vital role in the development of virtually all Anne Hébert's main characters. In *Le Premier jardin* in particular, her protagonist feels compelled to return to the area where she grew up in order to come to terms with a tragic event in her youthful past.

Outside the realm of fiction, childhood has frequently provided an analogy for Québec in writings treating social and political concerns. Editors of anthologies and authors of various general studies have sometimes found it useful to compare Québec as a national entity to a child. For example, in what seems to be almost an apology for his collection of essays purportedly representing "la pensée canadienne-française," Laurier LaPierre described Québec as grappling with "le problème de sa propre maturation." He maintains that one cannot expect cultural maturity from "une nation qui n'a pas atteint l'âge adulte dans les domaines politique et économique" (1967, 3). More recently and more optimistically, Ralph Sarkonak proclaims, "Long a land of silence inhabited by a people accused of lacking a history and a literature, Québec has, since the sixties, attained her cultural maturity, her *âge de la parole*" (1983, iii).

In his well-known and insightful essay, *Le Canadien-français et son double*, Jean Bouthillette compares Québec to a child abandoned by its mother. Referring to the Treaty of Paris, by which France ceded her colony to England in 1763, Bouthillette states, "La Conquête coupe trop tôt le cordon ombilical qui nous lie à la mère patrie." If this historical event had not taken place, Bouthillette postulates, Québec would have attained its natural maturity and eventually separated from France, much as the United States eventually gained its independence from England (1972, 24). It is possible that a connection between the frequent use of childhood as an analogy for Québec and the recurrent images of childhood in Québécois literature can be found in Bouthillette's assertion that profoundly debilitating feelings of loss and alienation have pervaded the collective consciousness since "la Conquête." Perhaps the sense of loss and alienation experienced by people separated irreparably from their homeland can be conveyed most poignantly and effectively through childhood imagery. Conceivably the process of defining a cultural identity and the steps toward achieving national autonomy can also be expressed and examined most thoroughly and naturally by means of allusions to childhood.

Writers representing many cultures have undoubtedly felt inspired to develop child protagonists for a variety of personal, political, and literary reasons. Most emerging nations have probably been referred to as infants. An emphasis on childhood cannot be attributed exclusively to Québécois writing, nor is Québec the only nation to have ever been compared to a child. Nevertheless, it is likely that childhood has been developed in Québécois literature in ways that express unique cultural realities. Indeed, Richard Coe has demonstrated convincingly that myths unique to individual cultures may be revealed and explored through the literary genre he describes as "the Childhood" (1984, 279). In his highly respected treatise on the roles and representations of children in society, Philippe Ariès claims to touch the "very heart of the great problems of civilization" (1962, 11). While it would be impossible to prove that certain perceptions or treatments of childhood pertain uniquely or specifically to Québec, "It is the process of searching that matters," as Patricia Smart has stated. She maintains that "the search for an answer" to the question of national specificity "has made it possible for us to hear the Canadian and Quebec voices in literature, to listen to them in their own terms and not according to the abstract, supposedly universal models to which we used to expect them to conform" (1987, 30). Exploring selected novels in which childhood stands out as a dominant theme, and investigating some of them in conjunction with other, more deliberately politically oriented Québécois writings, may illuminate some universal as well as some nationally specific social concerns, thereby promoting a greater understanding of Québécois society and its literary expression.

2
Paradise Lost
Nostalgic Reflections on Childhood in Novels by Gaspé, Conan, and Roquebrune

Québec's first novel, *L'Influence d'un livre*, by Philippe-Ignace-François Aubert de Gaspé, appeared in 1837. This work and virtually all Québécois novels published subsequently for the next hundred years are described as *romans de la fidélité* or *romans du terroir* because of their emphasis on "safeguarding the French-Canadian nationality, its customs, traditions and faith" (Shek 1977, 46). A well-known quotation from Louis Hémon's *Maria-Chapdelaine*, considered to be the epitome of regionalist works, sums up the message of "la survivance" conveyed by Québec's early novelists: "Au pays de Québec, rien ne doit mourir et rien ne doit changer" ([1914] 1931, 124). Since ethnic survival seemed possible only as long as Québécois families remained close to their land and true to their faith, members of the intellectual elite, such as Abbé Casgrain and Monsignor Camille Roy, encouraged novelists to base their works on edifying historical and rural themes. Maurice Cagnon notes that, in spite of their many adventures, characters in these novels undergo no real psychological evolution. Instead, "they stand as rigid monuments of good or evil." Further, "the omnipresent author never hesitates to underscore" the obvious "doctrinal or ideological stance" (1986, 9). Despite the blatant realities of industrialization and urbanization, Québec's writers, described by Arsène Lauzière as "modestes ouvriers" (1971, 1:179), conformed to pre-scribed guidelines and continued to promote preservation of traditional values well into the twentieth century.

Finally, a few novelists, such as Albert Laberge (*La Scouine*, 1918), Claude-Henri Grignon (*Un Homme et son péché*, 1933), Ringuet (*Trente arpents*, 1938), and Germaine Guèvremont (*Le Survenant*, 1945) turned a critical eye on agriculturist ideology by portraying the misery and hopelessness of protagonists whose values had become obsolete. These novelists, in the interest of realism, illustrate "l'échec d'un rêve, celui d'un Québec rural qui aboutissait à la prolétarisation d'une bonne partie de ses fils et de ses filles" (Lemieux 1984, 69).

Although Québec's leaders encouraged high birthrates as a means of promoting "la survivance," and although typical nineteenth-century rural families included an average of seven children (Lemieux 1984, 59), allusions to childhood rarely appear in the *roman du terroir*. In fact, children most often have the symbolic role of underscoring their father's conformity to social norms. In *La Terre paternelle* (1846), by Patrice Lacombe, for example, the protagonist finally settles down after a series of misadventures and provides his grateful parents with "des petits-enfants bien portants" (95). The evocation of healthy grandchildren assures the reader that all conflicts have been successfully resolved; order has been per-manently restored. In *Trente arpents*, one of the first novels to depict a large family, only the first son receives much atten-tion, and then only because his birth establishes Euchariste Moison officially as "époux et père, possesseur incontesté de cette terre faite sienne" (Ringuet 1938, 72). The son makes his next significant appearance in the novel as "un petit homme de onze ans" helping his father in the fields (81). While annual additions to Euchariste's family become part of the rural routine, the children themselves are not developed as characters.

Adult characters in the *roman du terroir* typically express nostalgia for their early years. However, their memories focus on the old family home, clearly a symbol of agrarian ideals, rather than on their actual childhood experiences, which are never described. The image of a kindly mother, "accueillante et consolatrice," patiently awaiting the return of her wayward offspring redoubles the ideological impact of "la vieille maison" (Lemieux 1984, 24). It is important to note that women have essentially the same nonrole as children in regionalist works. Their presence merely reinforces the social position of the male protagonist, whose interests dominate the narrative. The silent, capable wife produces a son to inherit patriarchal land and power; she and her other children labor quietly as respectful ancillaries. The *roman du terroir* clearly illustrates the ideology of "a male-centered hierarchy based in the Catholic Church and modelled on prerevolutionary France, where power descended in a direct line from God the Father to the King of France to the father of the family" (Smart 1987, 31).

Two nineteenth-century Québécois novels that stand out from a literary perspective, Philippe Aubert de Gaspé's *Mémoires* (1866), the first significantly successful attempt to record Québécois oral traditions (Falardeau 1972, 49), and Laure Conan's *Angéline de Montbrun* (1884), undisputedly "le roman le plus littéraire du siècle" (Lauzière 1971, 1:251), also contain the fullest, most interesting passages on childhood.

Gaspé's *Mémoires*, a collection of anecdotes formed into a fictionalized autobiography, and *Angéline de Montbrun*, Québec's first psychological novel written by Québec's first woman novelist, extol the same patriotism and religious values and depict the same traditional family structures as the *roman du terroir*. However, rather than insisting, like Maria Chapdelaine's father, that "rien ne changera, parce que nous sommes un témoignage" (Hémon [1914] 1931, 124), the narrators of these two novels concede the reality of change. Gaspé hopes that by consigning to future readers "des actions, des anecdotes, des scènes que mes soixante-dix-neuf ans me mettaient en mesure de transmettre à une nouvelle génération" (431), he might preserve a memory of the bygone

world in which he grew up. Laure Conan's protagonist meditates ruefully on her present state as well as on her past
throughout the final portion of *Angéline de Montbrun*. It has
been suggested that Laure Conan thinly disguised her own
autobiography in *Angéline de Montbrun* (Soeur Jean de l'Imaculée 1971, 109–11). Whether or not this is true, she was
certainly one of the first, if not the only, nineteenth-century
Québécois novelist to permit a protagonist to speak for herself
by writing her work in the first person. Gaspé also writes in
the first person, of course, because he is the main character in
his *Mémoires*. Both narrators, Gaspé and Angéline, acknowledge the present and the future as they attempt to understand
and establish continuity with the past. As they organize and
edit their recollections, childhood emerges as a central theme.

Robert de Roquebrune, a twentieth-century novelist and
historian, resembles Gaspé in his pressing need to preserve a
memory. In an interview, Roquebrune stated, "J'ai voulu
fixer sous une forme romanesque le souvenir de la civilisation
canadienne-française de jadis." Like Gaspé, he perceives his
writing as "une tentative de recréer une société disparue"
(Wyczynski 1971, 317). Roquebrune expands his recollections
into an entire novel about his childhood, *Testament de mon
enfance* (1958). He treats this topic in the same general terms
as Gaspé and Conan. Together, the three novelists define and
illustrate one of the distinctive patterns of treatment of childhood in Québécois literature.

Each narrator looks back on childhood as a perfect capsule
of paradise forever lost. Gaspé declares, "Je trouvais la vie
pleine de charme pendant mon enfance, ne m'occupant ni du
passé ni encore moins de l'avenir" (17). Comparing those days
to the present, he sighs, "Que les temps sont changés depuis
ma jeunesse!" (20). Roquebrune also describes his childhood
years as "une sorte d'éternité heureuse" lived out "dans la
plus profonde paix . . . dans le plus étonnant bonheur" (12).
In contrast, from his present perspective, "rien ne ressemble
plus à ce qu'était alors l'existence" (11). Angéline de
Montbrun similarly laments, "Beaux jours de mon enfance,

qu'êtes-vous devenus? . . . C'étaient vraiment les jours heureux" (121).

Loving, protective parents provide the blissful childhood environment described in all three novels. All of the parents are educated, comfortably wealthy members of the upper class who are well respected in the community. In each case, the father plays a lordly role in a social structure Janine Boynard-Frot aptly describes as feudal: "c'est l'image féodale du seigneur propriétaire de ses terres et de ses sujets" (1979, 44). Monsieur de Montbrun especially fits this description, since he has loyal "subjects" outside his immediate family in the local community. He secretly pays large debts on behalf of poor widows and teaches his daughter charity. Angéline recalls, "il me proposait toujours quelque infortune à soulager" (86). Monsieur Aubert de Gaspé, also highly esteemed in his parish, commands respect in his own household as his son attests, "Comment soutenir, en effet, son regard, quand il était courroucé ou qu'il affectait de l'être?" (65).

When distressing political or economic conditions preoccupy these exemplary fathers, their charming wives soon cajole them into good humor again. Roquebrune in particular comments on his mother's skill in influencing her husband's moods and decisions. As a prelude to discussing household finances, "elle s'approcha de mon père, passa tendrement son bras autour de ses épaules et l'entraîna au salon" (156–57). Angéline fulfills this function with "adorable coquetterie" (15) in the absence of her deceased mother.

Each narrator recalls being enveloped in a warm cocoon of loving attention. Angéline asserts that her father "voulait que je grandisse heureuse, joyeuse, . . . et pour cela il ne recula pas devant le sacrifice de ses goûts et de ses habitudes" (92). When Gaspé's mother threatens to punish her mischievous son, his confidence in her kindness dispells his worries: "je regardais la menace comme peu sérieuse." Certainly his mother "n'aurait jamais eu le coeur de faire coucher un de ses enfants sans souper" (65). Roquebrune stresses the love and protection he felt expressed in "tant de soins attentifs" (128).

In addition to attentive parents, a rural setting contributes a great deal to these three happy childhood experiences. All three families live in rather isolated manor houses surrounded by beautiful landscapes. Gaspé fondly recalls the trees "qui couronnent le beau promontoire qui s'élève au sud du domaine seigneurial" (20). Similarly, Roquebrune remembers his home "perdu en pleine campagne," as "un petit archipel composé du jardin, de la maison, d'un bois, d'un bout de rivière" (12). Angéline describes her family's garden: "Des noyers magnifiques ombragent ces belles eaux, et les fleurs sauvages croissent partout" (20).

The manor houses and their natural surroundings take on greater significance when one considers that each of the childhood experiences has a rural and an urban phase. Young Gaspé spends several blissful, innocent years at his family home, followed by a period of adventures and mischief while he is at boarding school in the city of Québec. Similarly, Angéline attends boarding school at the Ursuline convent in Québec after spending several years at home with her father personally supervising her studies. Roquebrune's entire family eventually moves to Montréal because his father accepts a position in the provincial government. The second, urban period is still considered part of the childhood experience in each case. Gaspé marks the end of his childhood when he finishes his studies in Québec and begins formal professional training with a lawyer. When Angéline is eighteen years old and has a serious suitor, her father insists that she is still a child, adding, "je désire beaucoup qu'elle reste enfant aussi longtemps que possible" (21). After his family's move to Montréal, Roquebrune still refers to himself as "un petit garçon de la ville" (173). Although still considered children after moving to an urban environment, all three narrators focus on their country homes when they evoke the idyllic moments of their childhood.

As children, each of the narrators seems to have spent much time alone in reverie. Angéline remembers musing about the night sky: "je voulais absolument qu'il y eût des trous dans le

plancher du ciel, par où on voyait la lumière de Dieu" (45–
46). Similarly, Gaspé reports, "Je me promenais seul, sur la
brune, de long en large dans la cour du manoir, et je trouvais
une jouissance infinie à bâtir de petits châteaux en Espagne"
(20). Roquebrune also relates, "Je passais des heures dans
une solitude peuplée de mes inventions" (147). As he remembers, taking the dogs and cats for an imaginary ride in a
dilapidated old carriage was preferable to playing with "le jeu
de flèches et mes soldats de plomb." He reflects, "Les gran-
des personnes ne comprennent pas les enfants et ne savent
pas que leurs plus beaux jouets sont toujours des objets bi-
zarres et nullement destinés au jeu" (147).

As a child, each narrator occasionally enjoyed the company
of one special friend. Angéline often joined her father's god-
child, the daughter of a poor fisherman: "Enfant, j'aimais la
société de cette petite sauvage qui n'avait peur de rien" (80).
Gaspé and Roquebrune each played with one of their broth-
ers. Gaspé recalls breaking a window on one occasion by
pressing his nose against the glass "en faisant des grimaces, à
travers les vitres à mon petit frère resté dans la maison" (63).
Roquebrune finds props in the attic for reenacting scenes from
history and literature with his older brother: "Je le suivais
avec une foi admirable dans son génie et j'acceptais toutes les
conventions de son sens dramatique" (55). Each narrator un-
derscores the significance of childhood by dwelling on the
nature of former games and pastimes.

In addition to descriptions of games and make-believe,
storytelling sessions figure prominently in each set of recollections. One of Gaspé's fondest memories is of being held by
the fire by visiting friars who tell him wonderful tales. He
declares, "Comme tous les enfants, j'aimais les légendes, les
contes et surtout les histoires de revenants les plus effroya-
bles" (337). Similarly, Roquebrune delights in the narrations
of his family's old servant, Sophronie. Unlike Gaspé, who
recalls details of the tales he heard, Roquebrune fills his
memory with the ambiance: "Je me souviens bien des soirées
dans la vieille cuisine, de nos visages tendus par l'intérêt, et

j'entends encore la voix de la conteuse" (37). In Angéline's family, even the adults enjoy fairy tales such as "Peau d'Ane." One of Angéline's friends from her convent school describes an evening she spent at the Montbrun home: "Tous les contes favoris de notre enfance y passèrent, et cette folle soirée fut la plus agréable du monde" (52).

Clearly, childhood is treated in Gaspé's *Mémoires*, in Conan's *Angéline de Montbrun*, and in Roquebrune's *Testament de mon enfance* as a joyful experience lived out in a beautiful, comfortable, love-filled environment. A move to an urban setting provides a brief transition before the realities of adult life relegate the childhood experience to the past. Much later, the narrators attempt to preserve in writing their memories of carefree childhood innocence.

Reflecting on the past can be bittersweet and sometimes painful. Memories of childhood evoke sadness both because a world perceived as perfect has vanished and because loved ones who were an important part of that world have passed away. Roquebrune particularly misses the old servants and his mentor, Jacques, who died in a hunting accident. Gaspé finds he has outlived most of his college companions, while Angéline mourns her father's sudden death.

Admittedly, Gaspé's recollections of his early life are little more than a context for his collection of legends and tales. Similarly, the memories Laure Conan attributes to her heroine Angéline are intended more to develop the latter's character than to describe her life as a little girl. Nevertheless, these two very different works offer glimpses of childhood in nineteenth-century Québec in a common glowing light. On the other hand, Roquebrune's *Testament de mon enfance*, written nearly a century later, gives full-scale expression to the same kinds of memories recorded in the two earlier works.

The childhood activities described in typical regionalist novels contrast sharply with those contained in the three novels dealing with more prosperous families. When children appear at all in the *roman du terroir*, they silently perform household duties, care for animals, and work in the fields. An exception may be found in Albert Laberge's *La Scouine* (1918), where the sordid amusements of some rural children are depicted with unsentimental realism. For example, on their way home from school, little boys habitually end their afternoon games "par un concours à qui pisserait le plus haut" (13). Cruel irony fills the few pages Laberge devotes to descriptions of childhood. Conversely, Conan, Gaspé, and Roquebrune, who focus on the children of families fortunate enough to have servants, evoke happy hours of wholesome playing and dreaming. Richard Coe observes that appreciation for the "apparently insignificant" child self requires a comparatively high degree of prosperity and cultural sophistication (1984, 15). Families descended from the old French nobility, such as those portrayed by Gaspé, Conan, and Roquebrune, have clearly met these criteria. Their children are valued as individuals; their childhood years are prolonged and pleasant.

The novels by Gaspé, Conan, and Roquebrune are related to the *romans de la fidélité* in that they uphold traditional moral and religious values and convey a glorified picture of country life. They are also nostalgic in tone, but theirs is not the vague melancholic longing that haunts typical regionalist works. On the contrary, their yearning focuses specifically on their childhood years. As they fondly recall selected events and people, Angéline, Gaspé, and Roquebrune communicate their conviction that childhood was the best part of life; nothing since has been particularly satisfying or interesting by comparison. An unmistakable tone of retrospective romanticism pervades the accurate records they purport to provide.

Madeleine Ducrocq-Poirier states that early novelists situated Québec's apogee "à l'arrière d'un passé où les Canadiens possédaient encore ce dont la conquête les avait dépouillés" (1978, 14). Her remark coincides with some of Jean Bouthillette's observations in his essay *Le Canadien-français et son double,* in which he maintains that an intense longing for "ce que nous avons été avant la présence anglaise" pervades Québec's collective consciousness (1972, 51). Of course, historians have suggested that the French colonial days were far from utopian. Pierre Guillaume, for example, states that "en 1763, la Nouvelle-France meurt de ses propres contradictions, non surmontées par la métropole, tout autant que de l'agression anglaise" (1984, 14). Bouthillette takes this perspective into account by implying that the French regime had to be revised and corrected before becoming a mythological "paradis perdu" (77). Since Gaspé, Conan, and Roquebrune treat childhood as a perfect period of peace and harmony irretrievably lost, and since childhood is undoubtedly also revised and corrected to some degree by narrators who recall few if any real difficulties or disappointments, it could be stated that works by Gaspé, Conan, and Roquebrune mirror a profound collective nostalgia for the idealized period prior to "la Conquête."

Further, Angéline de Montbrun's fictional life experience may be seen as a direct analogy for idealized Québécois history. Angéline as a child delighting in her beautiful natural surroundings can be taken as a figure for Québec in the early days as a French colony. Kindly Monsieur de Montbrun, who teaches his daughter to love books and provides her with a pious education, represents prerevolutionary France as a parent country, source of cultural and religious values and traditions. Angéline, like colonial Québec, contentedly accepts authority and remains protected. Tragically, the promise of a happy, prosperous future crumbles with Monsieur de Montbrun's sudden accidental death, analogous to "la Conquête." Poor Angéline becomes ill with grief and, mysteriously disfigured, alienates her fiancé. Her past happiness gone forever, her future ruined, she resembles Québec as an English acquisition viewed in mythological retrospect. Angéline resigns herself to a quiet, charitable life in her old home in the country. She spends her time meditating on religious themes and filling her journal with memories of her father and her childhood. Angéline's reclusion mirrors Québec's isolation and introspection during the years following "la Conquête." Her solitary courage and faithfulness to the past valorize Québec's persistent efforts to maintain cultural integrity. Conan communicates through Angéline "un regret diffus, une douleur inconsolée," which Bouthillette asserts are integral to the Québécois personality (51).

An analogy for Québec is certainly only one of many possible readings of *Angéline de Montbrun*. In recent years, a number of critical studies of Laure Conan's remarkable work have provided deeper insight into its complexity and surprising modernity. To cite a few examples, "Reflections in the Pool: The subtext of Laure Conan's *Angéline de Montbrun*" (1985), by François Gallays; "The Father's Seduction: The Example of Laure Conan's *Angéline de Montbrun*" (1986), by E. D. Blodgett; and "My Father's House: Exploring a Patriarchal Culture" (1987), by Patricia Smart, offer fresh perspectives on a novel that merits serious attention both as the first psychological novel published in Québec and as a precursor to an increasingly important and varied body of contemporary women's writing.

Times have changed since Gaspé, Conan, and Roquebrune committed to writing their impressions and memories of "the profoundly humane civilization of which all French Canada is heir" (Tougas 1976, 133). Parts of Bouthillette's interpretation of Québec's collective consciousness may no longer apply. Nevertheless, literary interest in childhood memories persists in Québec. Pierre Hébert suggests that the production of novels presented as "des variantes d'autobiographies fictives" has increased in recent years (1988, 900). Many contemporary fictionalized autobiographies, or novels presented as such, treat recollections of childhood with wistfulness and warmth, as earlier works do. Rural surroundings still provide the most propitious setting, although, through a child's eyes, city streets may also fill with magic. Much attention still is given to games and other imaginative pastimes. Family structures remain traditional and secure. Unlike their predecessors, contemporary novelists have the freedom to create works valid and pleasing in themselves; they may dispense with the moral or ideological subtext. For this reason, and also because they usually balance scenes of innocent bliss with some half-bemused accounts of childhood troubles and disappointments, readers may find contemporary works more plausible and more interesting than the earlier, romanticized recollections. Contemporary works tend to have a broader perspective. They permit the reader to discern signs of increasing maturity as the child self develops.

Roch Carrier is an example of a contemporary Québécois writer inspired, like Gaspé, to record oral traditions. Carrier's *Les Enfants du bonhomme dans la lune* (1979) contains a collection of anecdotes based on the author's own childhood, much like Gaspé's *Mémoires*. It is clear from Carrier's gentle vision of himself as a boy that he was happy, carefree, and loved. He had plenty of time to play and dream. In one of his anecdotes he describes how, as a child, he refused to believe that his mother bought new shoes for him from the village shoemaker. Instead, he insisted that an imaginary shoemaker in his attic had simply repaired his old ones while he slept. An older boy rudely interrupted as he explained this event to his envious classmates: "Un gros rire me frappa comme un coup au visage et brisa mon histoire" (18). At this break in his story, Carrier returns to his adult narrative perspective and meditates on the selective nature of memory. Unlike Gaspé, a traditional *conteur* who prides himself on perfect recall, Carrier admits that he remembers the imaginary shoemaker rather than the bombing of Hiroshima, which he knows must have filled the news at the same point in his past: "Ce trou de mémoire m'agace mais sans doute l'homme de choisit-il pas ce qui vient hanter sa mémoire" (19). Carrier wishes that everyone might have the good fortune to remember only happy events. In this spirit, he offers his own nostalgic recollections of the time before his worldview was marred by knowledge of war. Carrier received the Grand Prix Littéraire de la Ville de Montréal in 1980 for his collection of stories, which were widely known from radio broadcasts before they appeared in print. Continued appreciation for accounts of pleasant childhood memories marks one axis of contemporary Québécois literary expression.

3

Childhood in the City
Marie-Claire Blais's Pessimistic Vision

The years during which Maurice Duplessis served as Québec's prime minister, from 1936 to 1960 (with a brief interruption during World War II), are sometimes referred to in retrospect as *la grande noirceur,* or "the great darkness." M. L. Piccione characterizes Duplessis, whose personality dominates this period, as "un homme d'état autoritaire et un peu borné, qui maintenait le Québec dans l'infantilisme avec l'appui de forces rétrogrades" (1984, 253). In the shadow of Duplessis, a stifling ambiance of fear and apprehension seems to have pervaded Québec. Paul Emile Borduas enumerates the multiple facets of this paralyzing fear in his *Refus global* (1948): "Peur des préjugés—peur de l'opinion publique—des persécutions—de la réprobation générale; . . . peur de soi— de son frère—de la pauvreté; peur de l'ordre établi . . ." (1978, 47). Borduas was apparently premature in proclaiming the end of "la peur multiforme." After his *Refus global* appeared, he was relieved of his teaching position "pour avoir tenté de briser le silence." His expatriation constitutes "preuve flagrante que toute liberté de pensée était bannie du Québec duplessiste" (Piccione 1984, 252).

Although Gérard Tougas confirms that participation in World War II ended Québec's cultural isolation (1976, 147), and although some intellectuals, including Pierre Elliott Trudeau, attempted to break away from traditional thinking by starting the journal *Cité libre* in 1950, conservatism reigned until Duplessis's death in 1959. Liberal Jean Lesage's election in 1960 inaugurated a period of positive change known as "la Révolution Tranquille," or the Quiet Revolution.

Two events in particular characterize the changes that took place in Québec during the Révolution Tranquille. On one hand, the formation of Hydro-Québec in 1963 indicated Québec's intention to control its own natural and economic resources rather than to continue providing a passive labor force for English-Canadian and American capitalists. On the other hand, the creation in 1964 of a Ministry of Education to replace the traditional school system controlled by Catholic nuns and priests dramatically limited the Church's influence on society. A remarkable intellectual, cultural, and literary awakening accompanied these historical events (Guillaume 1984, 54).

Québécois authors of the 1960s frequently develop themes related to childhood misery in order to exorcise the darkness of past repression. Some of Marie-Claire Blais's works in particular express a vehement reaction against former spiritual and intellectual restraints. Her first novel, *La Belle bête*, appeared in 1959, when she was nineteen years old. Her open treatment of violence, murder, and incest was unusual for that time. In the years that followed, Blais continued to examine a world of dark misery, "brutal et opprimant, peuplé de nonnes sadiques et de prêtres dérangés, de rustres qui martyrisent leurs enfants et de prolétaires tuberculeux" (Atwood 1975, 21). Blais often chose to narrate from a child's innocent perspective to accentuate the intensely dark and corrupt atmosphere of her literary creation. Protagonists such as Jean-le-Maigre of her well-known *Une Saison dans la vie d'Emmanuel* (1965), Evans of *Tête blanche* (1960), and Pauline of *Manuscrits de Pauline Archange* (1968) are victims of the depravity they expose. Louise St. Pierre describes these characters as Blais's "enfants-témoins" (1969, 35).

In *Manuscrits de Pauline Archange,* Blais briefly develops the familiar theme of childhood as paradise lost. Her narrator, Pauline Archange, an adolescent who interprets her early years from the perspective of her more mature self, finds herself far from the bucolic tranquility evoked in earlier Québécois novels, however. On the contrary, Pauline and her best friend, Séraphine, experience all the effects of urban poverty. Since the children take refuge in their friendship, surmounting their difficulties with mutual support and affection, Pauline loses more than a playmate when a bus strikes and kills Séraphine. For Pauline, "le monde redevenait hostile, la nature perfide" following Séraphine's death (17). Pauline also grieves the loss of her childhood sense of innocence, wonder, and happiness when she laments, "Jamais cet été ne reviendra, ni l'été ni l'automne merveilleux où Séraphine jouait près de moi" (182). Pauline's narrative explores the wretched years that follow. Unloved and unwanted, cold and hungry in her noisy, dirty, and dangerous environment, Pauline rebels quietly and persistently against her passive, demoralized parents and the hypocritical nuns and priests who attempt to control her life. She affirms, "J'allais mon chemin, défiant une autorité que je jugeais monstrueuse" (19).

Maurice Cagnon observes that Blais has yet to portray "a lovable or even a healthy" family. He goes on to remark that "fathers, in particular, fail to provide support for and security of love to their children" (1986, 107). Absent, silent, and preoccupied, Pauline's father fits the pattern Cagnon describes. The little contact he has with Pauline is usually brutal, as her mother and school officials call upon him to punish his daughter for alleged misdeeds that hardly concern him. Pauline writes, "Il me frappa violemment pour en finir plus vite" (73). Thinking himself a model father, he waves proudly to the neighbors when he takes Pauline along as a reluctant passenger on his Sunday bicycle excursions. He remains nonetheless indifferent to all of her real needs and feelings. She rebels in the only way she can, by glaring at him through her clenched fists (83).

Monsieur Archange indeed represents "a traditional patriarchal order which preaches submission to authority and humiliation of body and spirit," as Mary Jean Green declares (1983, 132). We see him as both victim and perpetrator of this order. Although he feels exhausted by the menial jobs he performs day and night to maintain his family's meager existence, and although he feels "fini avant l'âge de quarante ans" (82), he remains complacent about his station in life. Having no ambition to better himself, he cares even less about the timid aspirations of his children. He frequently expresses admiration for his own tyrannical father, whom he dutifully imitates by exercising arbitrary authority over his own family, especially Pauline. He sends her to work at degrading jobs: "Mon père décidait brusquement 'qu'une fille de huit ans et demi' devait être utile à la société" (94). Her usefulness to society consists in selling wormy candied apples for her boorish uncle Roméo for twenty cents a day. More sadistically, he threatens to cut her education short: "Papa dit qu'après sa sixième année, une femme ça doit travailler comme ouvrière" (81). Since he cares little for intellectual pursuits, he views Pauline's constant reading and writing as a waste of time. He carelessly condemns her to a life as futile and as meaningless as his own.

Blais declines to make overt political statements, since she believes that "le dogmatisme stérilise l'écrivain." Instead, she prefers to "prendre position sur le plan moral" (Atwood 1975, 43). Thus, she perceives herself as a witness; she communicates her observations in writing and allows her readers to draw conclusions. It is possible for readers to understand through *Manuscrits de Pauline Archange* a criticism of social structures and conditions in Québec during *la grande noirceur*.

Following his death, Duplessis was seen by many as "une véritable incarnation du mal" (Piccione 1984, 253), as if all of Québec's social and political problems could be blamed on him. Duplessis has been compared to a father figure representing the same traditional structures and causing the same hindrance to progress as Monsieur Archange. His rather dictatorial administration favored agriculturalism, discouraged free thinking, and allowed English-Canadian and American

capitalists to exploit Québec's labor force and natural resources (Guillaume 1984, 53–54), much as Monsieur
Archange would have stifled his daughter's ambitions and
relegated her to a harsh, hopeless, proletarian existence.

Blais does not stop with Monsieur Archange in her criticism
of patriarchal structures. She also portrays Pauline's mother as
a victim of the system she serves. Pauline states that her
mother "désirait pour nous ce qu'elle avait jadis souhaité pour
elle-même, une existence fière" (82). Disillusioned by the
impossibility of realizing her dreams, Madame Archange
rejects her life and circumstances symbolically through frequent vomiting, which leaves her too weak to care properly for
her children. Pauline complains, "ma mère m'oubliait des
jours entiers" (80).

Helpless to change her unhappy situation, Madame Archange nevertheless devoutly upholds the religious beliefs that
keep her ill and impoverished as she dutifully bears more
children. She strives to instill her own patient submission,
passive suffering, fear, and guilt in her family. Ironically,
Madame Archange becomes so preoccupied with the state of
her soul that she fails to notice her confessor's sexual abuse of
Pauline. She would never suspect such reprehensible behavior from "le mystique Franciscain aux regards indiscrets,"
who represents for her "la religion en personne" (46). As
defense against the onslaughts of her mother's religious im-
positions, Pauline artfully postpones returning home from
school to study her catechism: "Je m'en fuyais en allant jouer
dans la rue" (110). Later, forced to memorize the required
responses, she redoubles her mental rebellion: "tout mon être
y résistait comme à un pouvoir malsain" (46).

St. Pierre points out that mothers in Blais's novels consistently serve as "défenseurs des valeurs morales" (90). Soeur
Sainte-Marie-Eleuthère confirms the accuracy of Blais's por-
trayals when she states that the Québécois mother traditionally constituted "l'auxiliaire la plus généreuse et la plus
dévouée" of the priest, "gardien de la foi et de la race" (1971,
197). Blais criticizes the Church extensively in *Manuscrits de*

Pauline Archange by portraying deviant, depraved nuns and priests who commit heinous acts against children. In addition, she uses her protagonist's perspective to protest against the part mothers have played in furthering religious oppression. Madame Archange certainly resigns herself to her prescribed role in life, thinking herself unworthy to question, confessing her minutest sins. She in turn burdens her daughter with a legacy of repressive teachings.

Occasionally Pauline perceives "une soeur incomprise" in her mother, but she quickly represses feelings of pity or tenderness by submerging her thoughts in icy reverie (25). Green remarks that Pauline's rejection of her mother stems from an "innate refusal to identify with those who are condemned to be victims" (131). Thus, Pauline instinctively distances herself emotionally from her mother's world of patient suffering as a necessary step in obtaining her own freedom. Pauline's rejection of her mother as a pathetic victim of the strictest Catholicism implies a strong reaction against the Church's insidious impact on her own life.

In spite of Pauline's resistance, Madame Archange succeeds in imbuing her daughter with a deep sense of moral guilt. She undermines Pauline's self-esteem by scolding continually, "Ah! T'es ben méchante, la Pauline" (72), and "T'as donc pas de coeur, la Pauline? . . . Ah! t'as jamais été bonne" (43). At school, the nuns threaten Pauline with an image of God's eye scowling at her misdeeds: "Ce regard partout vous regarde et vous guette" (15). When Pauline, overcome by temptation, steals a small sum from her cousin Cécile, her remorse takes on far greater proportions than warranted by her misdeed because of her deeply ingrained sense of guilt and unworthiness: "Mon vol brûlait ma conscience comme le souvenir d'un crime" (95). More tragically, Pauline feels guilty about imagined sins. She takes personal responsibility for her friend Séraphine's death: "Je l'avais volontairement perdue" (42). She believes she personally failed her handicapped cousin Jacob when adults commit him to an asylum. Echos of his unfair accusations plague her conscience: "J'm'en vais en enfer, la cousine, la Pauline tu m'aimes donc pas, tu m'as pas gardé, j'm'en vais" (75). She also blames herself for her disabled brother's suffering, believing that his pain somehow expiates her sins (107). Condemning herself, she envies angelic Séraphine, "qui est déjà au paradis" (99).

Clearly, Pauline's sense of culpability has been cultivated by the rigid Catholic ideology permeating her thoughts and her environment, with its much greater emphasis on condemnation than on forgiveness. Blais develops the theme of Catholic guilt in other works, including her play, *L'Exécution* (1968). Jennifer Waelti-Walters discusses the implications of guilt in her study of this drama, noting that the conflict between aspiring to higher moral values and feeling perpetually condemend as a hopeless sinner is enough "to incapacitate any thinking individual." Waelti-Walters interprets *L'Exécution* as a "revolt against the Roman Catholic church and an indictment of its hold over society, a society reduced to powerlessness by the opposing nature of the demands made daily upon each of its members" (1981, 51).

Jean Bouthillette confirms the predilection for religious guilt prevalent in Québécois society in his essay *Le Canadien-français et son double,* suggesting that such feelings actually stem from a deeper national malaise that can be traced back to "la Conquête." He states, "notre sentiment de l'échec s'est culpabilisé. . . . Nous sommes à la fois dépossédés et coupables de l'être" (1972, 72). Bouthillette contends that combined national and religious feelings of guilt pervade every aspect of life in Québec (74). Blais's work explores the manifestations and consequences of deep-seated, debilitating guilt. Her protagonist, Pauline Archange, experiences symptoms of the culpability Bouthillette and Waelti-Walters examine and deplore in Québécois society as a whole.

Pauline's problems are compounded by suffocating feelings of boredom and despondency. She endures her uninspiring classes "en soupirant d'ennui" (83). Knowing instinctively that her education, such as it is, constitutes her only hope for better circumstances, she weeps with despair when she achieves high marks simply by being slightly less mediocre than the others (114). Pauline's clothing reflects her poor self-image: "J'étais seule et indigne d'être aimée dans ma robe en lambeaux" (114). Depression prevents her from taking action to improve herself: "toute transformation de moi-même me semblait futile" (114). Further, her father reminds her that she was not born to fulfill her dreams. He evokes the Québécois saying "né pour un petit pain," a reminder not to struggle against fate.

Again, Pauline's mental outlook reflects the emotions Bouthillette attributes collectively to Québec: "un pessimisme profond, une lassitude déprimante, un sentiment insondable d'impuissance" (91). Pauline's efforts to overcome her paralyzing sense of futility mirror her nation's collective struggle.

As a child in an urban proletarian family, Pauline derives little inspiration from her environment. She complains about her lack of books (96). A nun confiscates the few volumes she does manage to obtain, along with her diaries and poems. Pauline remarks bitterly, "Pourquoi aurions-nous le droit de rendre fertile notre paysage intérieur, le droit de penser et même de vivre, quand elle, depuis son entrée au couvent, a renoncé à toute espérance, à toute vanité?" (101). Pauline regrets that her intellect remains constantly in chains (28).

The censure of books and personal papers was apparently a common feature of strict convent school discipline. Protagonists in other novels, such as Claire Martin's *Dans un gant de fer* (1965), share Pauline Archange's complaints. They express the rebellion thousands of little girls and young women must have felt against a system designed to prepare them for a life of sacrifice and self-abnegation as model Catholic wives and mothers. In their thoroughly researched and illuminating study, *Les Couventines* (1986), Micheline Dumont and Nadia Fahmy-Eid soberly underscore the severity of rules and rigid restrictions with which young women were forced to comply if they hoped to receive any education at all. They emphasize, "Il faut bien se rendre à l'évidence que le pensionnat a constitué, durant près d'un siècle, le seul lieu où il était possible à une fille d'obtenir de l'instruction et, avec l'instruction, un espoir d'aspirer à une vie différente" (20). While the limitations imposed on young women were unequivocably greater than those imposed on young men, the conditions about which Pauline protests nevertheless reflect the Church's overall traditional approach to intellectual activity in Québec. As Dumont has stated, "l'emprise de l'Eglise québécoise s'est exercée de façon totalitaire jusqu'au début des annés 1960." She adds, "la doctrine sociale de l'Eglise a constitué le corridor étroit dans lequel les fidèles devaient cheminer s'ils voulaient assurer le salut de leur âme" (20). Borduas attests that priests were viewed as "seuls dépositaires de la foi, du savoir, de la vérité et de la richesse nationale." As such, they protected their flock from "l'évolution universelle de la pensée pleine de risques et de dangers," distorting facts when they were unable to enforce "l'ignorance complète" (1978, 45). In Blais's work, the nuns' seizure of books could also be seen as a criticism of the Church's former control of literary production. Denise Lemieux reminds us that Abbé Casgrain edited Québec's first novel prior to its printing: "il enlève des citations, remplace le mot amour par le mot amitié ou affection, supprime un juron" (1984, 17). Nearly a century later, Jean-Charles Harvey's *Les Demi-Civilisés* (1934), now considered to be a classic, was indexed, to name only one well-known example of prolonged and widespread censorship of literature.

Pauline and her friends ache with wondering what will become of their lives (83). Their question conveys an urgent adolescent need to develop a strong personal identity and to establish clear personal goals. Their anxiety also reflects Québec's national concern with cultural identity. Bouthillette believes that adopting the name "Québécois," which expresses the full reality of his nation's true identity, to replace "French Canadian," which implies duality and ambiguity, was an essential step toward establishing "le peuple québécois" as a cultural group seeking, "dans son nationalisme décolonisateur," full political expression (96). A vital issue during the Révolution Tranquille, the development and expression of this collective identity, continues to be explored in Québécois literature.

Writing is Pauline's first step toward working out and fully experiencing her personal identity. In the strictly imposed evening solitude of her boarding school, she gradually collects and assembles the fragments of her life (96). Having committed the "choses noires" of her past to writing, she can free herself from them by creating a new narrative for her future. She states, "née dans le récit même que je voulais écrire, j'aspirais seulement à en sortir" (127). Writing constitutes a crucial act of self-determination. In addition, it provides insurance against the threat of nonexistence. Pauline suspects that "sans ces quelques pages, je risquais de n'avoir existé pour personne" (127).

Piccione regards writing as one of the principal themes of Québécois novels since the Révolution Tranquille. She remarks, "l'écriture devint alors déterminante, à la fois témoignage et pamphlet, exorcisme et thérapie." Further, she observes that the vast majority of protagonists maintain a personal journal or propose to write a novel of their own (269). Pauline Archange thus, like other characters in Québécois novels of the 1960s, betrays her creator's preoccupation with literary expression.

Mlle Léonard, a bright young doctor who volunteers her services at the convent school, provides a positive role model for Pauline. Impressed by Mlle Léonard's intelligence and dignity, Pauline is touched by the doctor's interest in her. As she states, for the first time "quelqu'un était là" (88). Blais emphasizes Mlle Léonard's importance as "un personnage de grande dimension," who is truly "libérée," "généreuse," and "libératrice" (Marcotte 1983, 202). When nuns prevent Mlle Léonard, a professed atheist, from providing much-needed health care at their school, her continued sincere concern for Pauline brings to mind the words of Borduas: "Par-delà le christianisme nous touchons la brûlante fraternité humaine"

(46). Mlle Léonard can be seen as a representative of Québec's emerging self-image in the Révolution Tranquille. She is as Bouthillette wishes Québec to become, "jeune, moderne, enraciné et ouvert au monde" (96).

One might wonder if the dreary world portrayed through Pauline's eyes is not exaggerated, especially since darkness generally characterizes Blais's work. As Cagnon declares, her novels "explore troubled worlds, disturbing characters, situations that range from the vaguely unpleasant to the utterly hopeless" (1986, 106). Vincent Nadeau confirms that "d'un roman à l'autre, également, la noirceur est reprise et explorée" (1974, 11). Blais is not, however, the only Québécois author to portray childhood in sordid terms. Claire Martin, for one, states in *Dans un gant de fer*, "Je ne sais pas à quel âge j'ai compris que, là où j'étais née, le bonheur ne serait pas mon lot" (1965, 11). Similarly, Anne Hébert's François begins his narration in *Le Torrent*, "J'étais un enfant dépossédé du monde" (1965, 9). The reality of darkness in Québécois society during "la grande noirceur" is emphasized by Madeleine Greffard, who attests that Blais's *Une Saison dans la vie d'Emmanuel* accurately translates "une saison dans la vie d'un peuple." Greffard further affirms, "Marie-Claire Blais nous a donné dans ce roman l'expression la plus mûre, la plus puissante et la plus objective de notre vie" (1966, 24).

Pierre Vallières's highly influential essay, *Nègres blancs d'Amérique* (1967), published one year prior to *Manuscrits de Pauline Archange*, contains similar scenes of working-class life in Québec during the Duplessis administration. Vallières records his own childhood experiences as a sort of justification for his militant political manifesto. He attests to a very real personal struggle, which he believes many shared. His depiction of economic depression and despair reinforces Blais's critical observation of social conditions. Vallières's perception of his parents is distinctly different from that of Pauline Archange, however, and provides an opportunity to investigate another aspect of Québécois cultural mythology.

As a child, Vallières escapes "l'enfer familial" (104) by

playing in the streets, much as Pauline Archange flees the "douloureux tableau" (110) of her home life. Like her, he foments silent insurgence: "m'efforçant de ne rien entendre autour de moi, j'écoutais ma révolte qui montait et réchauffait mon sang" (81). He shares Pauline's low self-esteem, assessing himself as "petit, chétif, pauvre, mal vêtu, mal élevé, ignorant" (164), as well as her urgent quest for identity and purpose: "Je voulais faire quelque chose, devenir quelqu'un" (164). Like Pauline, Vallières preoccupies himself with writing: "je décidai qu'un jour j'écrirais un livre sur ma famille, mon milieu social, ma faim de liberté et de justice" (174).

Jacques Ferron, an altruistic doctor, writer, and politician, serves as a role model for young Vallières, much as Mlle Léonard guides Pauline Archange. Ferron offers Vallières compassion, inspiration, and political tracts.

Monsieur Vallières, like Monsieur Archange, works long hours to support his family. As a result, he also appears exhausted and ruined at an early age (82). Vallières complains that he suffered from his father's absence (141). He perceives "un mélange d'immense bonté, de silencieuse souffrance" in his father's eyes and feels his solidarity even though they rarely communicate verbally (81). Vallières shares his father's unspoken belief "que ses rêves étaient réalisables" (81) so strongly that he dedicates *Nègres blancs d'Amérique* to his memory.

In contrast, Vallières execrates his mother as a neurotic, domineering woman solely responsible for her family's miserable condition. He especially blames her for his father's unhappiness, insisting that if only she had been more courageous, "mon père aurait mieux vécu et donné un sens à sa vie" (107). Instead, fearing changes that might threaten her fragile security, she discourages her husband from involvement in political activities.

In *Manuscrits de Pauline Archange*, both parents are portrayed more or less equally as victims and as perpetrators of rigid social structures and oppressive religious teachings. They seem to contribute mutually to their misery, both fearing change, both caught in the web of darkness Borduas describes in his *Refus global*. Pauline rejects them both equally. She seeks freedom from patriarchal order in all its manifestations.

Vallières, in contrast, portrays his father as an innocent victim whose life consists in "une routine faite d'humiliations silencieusement subies, d'inutile soumission au bon plaisir de sa femme inquiète" (107). Perhaps his emasculation reflects Québec's devalued ethnicity. Bouthillette suggests that Québec as a nation, once healthy and virile, became "petit, frileux, mesquin, peureux, veule et lâche" under English domination (91–92). Vallières asserts his own virility and vindicates his father by engaging in strong political action. He affirms a strong, new determination on the part of Québec's workers to take control of their economic and political lives and thus "transformer en une société plus juste et plus fraternelle ce pays, le Québec" (21).

As he reviles his mother, Vallières also denounces the Church, her ally, as the ultimate "Mother of mothers." By resisting change in her own small sphere of influence, Madame Vallières dutifully contributes her efforts to the Church's campaign to maintain tradition. Vallières holds his mother responsible for her husband's lack of will just as he blames religious indoctrination for breaking Québec's collective spirit. Vallières fears and rejects his mother as well as the Church as vicious castraters. In order to assert his freedom and masculinity, Vallières vociferously censures his mother and the values she represents.

Soeur Sainte-Marie-Eleuthère confirms the notion that, by virtue of their association with the Church, mothers represent in literature and in the collective consciousness "tout ce dont nous avons hérité avec la race: la foi, la langue, les traditions, et aussi les préjugés, le conformisme, certaines étroitesses d'esprit" (1971, 204). To the extent that these legacies are perceived as liabilities, revolt consists in rejection of the mother. Piccione employs a similar analogy in stating that rebellion against the Church was an essential step for Québec to "dépasser sa condition de Fils et accéder au statut d'Homme" (262).

Vallières's autobiographical political essay is a personal testimony that reflects general attitudes in Québec during the 1960s. While he proclaims his own misogyny vociferously throughout his discussion of family life, he does allude to miserable conditions in a way that lends credibility to Blais's fictional account of childhood in *Manuscrits de Pauline Archange*. Vallières's writing confirms the accuracy of Blais's dark and depressing vision.

Blais illustrates in *Manuscrits de Pauline Archange* the "blocus spirituel" described by Borduas in his *Refus global* (45). She sets a dark, fear-filled scene in which her characters turn in circles, "comme des insectes avides à la faible lumière de leur dégoût" (17). Her young protagonist observes the most oppressive aspects of urban Québec during *la grande noirceur*. By recording her sordid memories, Pauline hopes to free herself from the "trous noirs et vides" (17). Through Pauline, Blais emphasizes writing as a means of self-determination. Her concern is shared by Vallières and by many other authors who contributed to Québec's literary explosion during the 1960s. Blais's narrator and Vallières use writing about their beginnings as a crucial step in working their way out of hopeless darkness.

The vehement manner in which Duplessis and the Church are denounced in works such as Blais's and Vallières's, as well as in essays by Borduas and Bouthillette, among others, evokes the rebellion of a teenager attempting to break free from parental authority. Comparisons of Québec to a child or adolescent are prevalent in a variety of writings, as are allusions to Duplessis and the Church as parents. These authority structures, according to Vallières, kept Québec in the Middle Ages until the 1960s. Autonomy from them had to be gained before Québec could leap into the twentieth century and "come of age" (15).

Blais uses a fictional childhood to comment on social conditions during the Duplessis administration. Pauline's youthful perspective enables the reader to draw critical conclusions concerning patriarchal authority, Church-controlled education, and the effects of general corruption and depravity on a young mind. Once she has called forth and exorcised the past, Blais ends her work on a more positive note. Pauline's determination to overcome all obstacles to freedom signals an end to the "règne de la peur multiforme" (Borduas 1978, 46), both for her own fictional life and for Québec as a whole.

In an interview in 1975, Blais acknowledged that the Québec she described in *Manuscrits de Pauline Archange* no longer existed. She stated that Québec, thanks to economic progress and educational reform, had become "un pays palpitant où il fait bon vivre" (Atwood 1975, 46).

4

Childhood as an Intellectual Adventure

Jacques Ferron and Louise Maheux-Forcier

In Jacques Ferron's *L'Amélanchier* (1970), translated as *The Juneberry Tree* (1975), Tinamer de Portanqueu narrates her memories of childhood in Québec both for the pure pleasure of recalling the past and, more importantly, in order to take her bearings. She remarks that, as a solitary traveler set adrift, her only reliable point of reference is the fixed star of her childhood (11). Her recollections permit her to reaffirm her identity and to establish her direction and purpose in life.

Tinamer's early memories remain inseparable from her own "domaine enchanté," a small, heavily wooded acreage located just beyond her family's garden. As an adult reviewing the setting of her childhood experience, she recognizes that its topography exists both within her and outside of her. Parts of the actual landscape either always were or later became imaginary. Situated at the heart of her youth, and thus subject to distortions of memory, her domain gradually expanded in proportion and significance, "d'une maison devenant comté, d'un comté pays" (142–43). Tinamer repeatedly alludes to her childhood domain as her own country, her personal homeland. She observes that her father also has a childhood country about which he reveals few concrete details. Tinamer understands his reticence in spite of her curiosity: "c'était le pays de son enfance, son pays particulier qu'il ne pouvait livrer" (79). In growing up, Tinamer internalized her childhood world, so that the real and mythical place now exists for her only, as an integral part of herself. She states, "je ne saurais me dissocier de ces lieux sans perdre une part de moi-même" (11). Her efforts to call forth her memories of childhood and its domain and to organize and record her recollections become for her a process of self-discovery.

The notion of a collective homeland that is as much a part of a people as the personal childhood domains are of its individual members constitutes a dominating and recurring theme of Ferron's work. Maurice Cagnon maintains that all of Ferron's novels feature characters whose actions center around "future possession of self and country." Cagnon further notes that Ferron's fiction is firmly grounded in Québécois reality and that the existence of Québec as an "an autonomous political and social identity" persistently "comprises the raw material" for his writing (1986, 84).

Jean Bouthillette uses imagery similar to Ferron's when he declares, "c'est au pays de l'enfance oubliée qu'il nous faut encore revenir" (1972, 70). Bouthillette proposes a reaffirmation of past history as a means of resolving the contradictions and ambiguities he sees as undermining Québec's future as a nation. Ferron's *L'Amélanchier*, in part, illustrates the urgency and importance Bouthillette attaches to establishing a clearly defined ethnic identity.

Tinamer's childhood domain has some characteristics that associate it more or less closely with Québec. In Tinamer's personal mythology, her woods are actually the property of an Italian who purchased the land from an Englishman. Québec also, of course, became English territory subsequent to "la Conquête" and was also subject to control by the Catholic church, alluded to irreverently in Tinamer's narrative as the "prélats italiens" (113). Actual ownership being a moot point, Tinamer's father declares himself content with the right to simply use and enjoy the land. Besides, the enchanted domain with which Léon de Portanqueu endows his daughter is

far more vast than its legal dimensions would imply (24).
Léon passes on to Tinamer all of Québec's traditional agri-
cultural values when he demonstrates his profound respect for
the earth, treating it as something extremely precious. He
teaches her that "il n'y a rien de plus beau . . . que le travail
de l'homme marié à la générosité de la terre maternelle" (95).
Further, Léon promises that someday he will take Tinamer
away to the land where he himself grew up: "nous traver-
serons le bois, nous franchirons le lac et nous irons vivre tous
les deux ensemble dans ce beau comté où je suis né" (29).
The dreamlike attraction of the distant "comté de Mask-
inongé" evokes Jack Warwick's well-known study of *L'Appel
du nord dans la littérature canadienne-française* (1972), especially
considering that Léon's mythical territory "s'étendait vers le
nord, à l'infini" (29). Léon also teaches Tinamer about her
family's illustrious lineage, which can be traced back as far as
"le déluge" (when their French ancestors crossed the Atlantic). Tinamer considers knowledge of her origins to be sacred.
Léon bases her religious instruction on readings from a special
Bible containing family legends in lieu of those related in
"l'autre" Bible, "celle de tout le monde" (68). Québec's oral
traditions clearly inspire the colorful history of Tinamer's
clan. Elements of Québec's cultural heritage permeate Tinamer's early childhood environment to the point that her
fictional homeland and Québec itself could be taken as one
and the same. As Pierre L'Hérault phrases it, "le texte ferro-
nien apparaît comme la mise en forme particulière d'une
sagesse commune. Il constitue le récit organisé d'une rêverie
collective" (1980, 214).

Once Tinamer begins attending school, she abandons both
the physical and imaginary aspects of her childhood domain.
Previously, her father took care to make the woods seem
immense: "à tourner, à retourner, à faire des ronds et des
huit, nous pouvions marcher à notre saoul, des heures et des
heures" (94). Now, in the company of her new peers, Tinamer soon discovers an area where trees have been cleared to
permit the construction of homes. With her new perspective,

her childhood land seems very small indeed (111). Further, to her surprise and dismay, she learns facts at school that contradict all her father's legends and explanations. Taking her academic success as "preuve que tout ce qu'on m'apprenait était vrai" (111), she resents her father, "un sacré farceur," for having made fun of her (113). Recalling her eagerness to learn more and to make a place for herself in the world, she remarks regretfully, "j'avais hâte, pauvre moi, d'être plus grande encore" (112).

During the period following World War II and into the beginning of the Révolution Tranquille, there was a tendency in Québec to abandon traditions and to reject the past in favor of modernity and progress. Denouncing values represented by the aspergillum and the wool cap of the habitant, Paul Emile Borduas exclaims in his *Refus global:* "Au diable le goupillon et la tuque!" (1978, 46). Similarly, Pierre Vallières cries out in *Nègres blancs d'Amérique,* "Brûlons le carton-pâte des traditions avec lequel on a voulu mythifier notre esclavage" (1967, 24). Bouthillette confirms that the postwar generation rejected its cultural heritage, along with the rigid concept of nationalism associated with the Duplessis era, in order to embrace contemporary socioeconomic reality. He deplores the loss of identity inherent in this approach, which he views as an escape "dans le non-pays de l'homme sans visage" (1972, 62).

Ferron stresses the importance of identity and its relationship to childhood in a key passage of *L'Amélanchier:* "l'enfance est avant tout une aventure intellectuelle où seules importent la conquête et la sauvegarde de l'identité" (49). Tinamer's identity is deeply rooted in the woods that become her personal homeland. She compares herself to the beautiful, flowering juneberry tree and to the native woodcock, "la bécasse du Canada," that thrive in her enchanted land. A revelatory dream that permits Tinamer to establish her identity takes place in these surroundings.

The dream sequence plays a crucial role in the development of Tinamer's memory. As a child, Tinamer observed with fear and annoyance that when she awakened in the morning she had absolutely no recollection of the previous day. Fortunately, familiar surroundings helped her recall her identity. If by chance she were to awaken somewhere else, she might quite possibly not know herself: "je risquais de ne pas me retrouver, devenue une petite fille sans nom et sans raison" (49). As long as she relied on her parents and her environment to reestablish her precarious identity each morning, she remained a child (39). The vivid dream carried her memory through the night for the first time, marking the birth of her own autonomous self.

Tinamer's father relates an incident from his own childhood that reinforces the significance of Tinamer's discovery. He recalls that, as a child, he retained each morning only a dreamlike impression of the previous day, "comme si j'avais dormi depuis ma naissance" (63). Once, however, he awakened to hear the nearby parish church burning. This event, the equivalent of Tinamer's dream, permitted his memory to span the night. He explains, "enfin je me trouvais réuni à moi-même, capable de continuité par mes seuls moyens" (67).

Tinamer's father believes in the vulnerability of all children who happen to wake up in a new place before developing enough internal memory to bridge the night. He works at a mental hospital for children who have become lost in this way. When Tinamer outgrows the stories he shared with her, he gently and patiently uses them to build an identity for a lost little boy.

Tinamer's dream reveals some subliminal conflicts in her relationship with her parents at the same time it allows her to gain some independence from them. On the whole, Tinamer relates to her parents comfortably, in a relaxed, affectionate manner. She calls her father by his first name. For her, when he is draped in an old burnoose, a relic from the Iroquois massacre of settlers at Lachine in 1689, he good-naturedly represents the past. Tinamer eventually mistakes the man himself for "une vieillerie" (94). After her dream, in which

Léon, disguised as a satyr, presides over strange revels, Tinamer recognizes that she belongs to a different "confrérie" from him. Instead of identifying exclusively with him and their pet dog, her "brother," she begins to understand her mother, for whom she previously felt antipathy.

Tinamer calls her mother Etna because she once lost her patience and exploded like a volcano. Efficient, hardworking, and self-effacing, Etna fulfills a traditional maternal role in Tinamer's narrative. Tinamer's antagonism toward her mother surfaces in an occasional skirmish and in her dream where Etna appears as an evil bird. Thinking herself unattractive with her dark hair cut short like a boy's, especially compared to her delicate imaginary friend Mary Mahon, Tinamer accuses her mother of making her resemble a silly woodcock. Both Etna and the phantom Messire Hubert Robson, who inhabits the enchanted woods and who shares Etna's kind look and love for children, reassure her that she is indeed "très jolie et gentille" (97). Tinamer's acceptance of her appearance and of her female identity reflects in her enhanced appreciation for Etna. She eventually admits, "je n'éprouvais plus d'antipathie à son égard. Je la trouvais même plaisante et chaleureuse" (102).

An additional result of her dream is that Tinamer becomes obsessed with a sense of time pulling her forward by a long feather or thread attached to the end of her nose. Always looking eagerly ahead, she realizes, "mes années d'insouciance ont coulé comme l'eau" (137). At the age of twenty, Tinamer suddenly feels terribly alone, strangely invisible to herself, and overshadowed by a premonition of death (147).

The images Tinamer uses to describe her crisis call to mind passages in which Bouthillette suggests that, having abandoned its "terres idylliques," much as Tinamer outgrew her enchanted domain, Québec, like Tinamer, drifts aimlessly in a dreary, faded world (67). Bouthillette describes the people of Québec as "devenus illisibles à nos propres yeux, dépossédés et livrés à nos solitudes isolées" (55). Similarly,

Tinamer's hesitation "entre le goût de vivre et celui de mourir" (143) brings to mind Bouthillette's assertion that Québec must overcome "cette sournoise tentation de la mort" (97) in order to continue existing as a vital ethnic entity. Jean-Marc Léger concurs with Bouthillette when he affirms that, "le Québec, à l'aube de 1969, est atteint d'une profonde mélancolie et qu'il paraît frappé d'une sorte d'impuissance à se déterminer, à s'orienter" (1983, 349).

Instinctively, in spite of the taut thread of time pulling her forward, Tinamer turns himself around and, looking backward, finds her childhood world intact. She instantly regains her lost identity: "je me revoyais, je me retrouvais" (147–48). Thus, as Jean-Pierre Boucher has stated, "le récit de son enfance n'est donc pas une fin en soi mais l'étape essentielle qui mènera Tinamer à la découverte de son identité personnelle et du sens à donner à sa vie" (1973, 16). Boucher further observes that Tinamer's account of her childhood serves the same purpose as her dream. "Par l'exercice de la mémoire qu'il implique," her narrative takes her back across the years of oblivion just as the dream preserved her precarious childhood identity through the night (24). Of course, Tinamer cannot remain facing backward, any more than as a child she could have continued living in her dream. Nevertheless, her brief return to vital sources suffices to establish her identity, to permit reorientation of her life, and to provide courage, inspiration, and purpose.

In the final chapter of his essay, Bouthillette states his conviction that Québec's history will right itself as soon as the people of Québec establish a firm identity by putting the past in perspective (95). According to Bouthillette, replacing the ambiguous double identity of "Canadien-français" with the more accurately descriptive name "Québécois" constituted a vital step in affirming Québec's national sovereignty (96).

Boucher warrants that *L'Amélanchier*'s structure presents "une homologie frappante avec celle de la société québécoise en 1970," in that "au moment même où la société québécoise cherche son identité nationale," the novel "nous présente des personnages précisément à la recherche de leur identité" (101).

Ferron's portrayal of Tinamer's personal search for identity clearly reflects contemporary Québécois concerns. As Ferron traces Tinamer's quest, he evokes Québec's unique sources of identity: both Tinamer and Québec have deeply established roots in history, in a specific geographical location, and in oral tradition. Tinamer's instinctive return to her sources for purpose and orientation corresponds to Québec's collective appeal to memory, reflected in the motto adopted during the Révolution Tranquille, "Je me souviens."

Ferron's evocation of the past as a source of identity is paralleled by another novelist, Louise Maheux-Forcier, in *L'Ile joyeuse* (1964). Much like Ferron's Tinamer de Portanqueu, Maheux-Forcier's protagonist, Isabelle, regains her lost identity through the recollection of certain pivotal childhood experiences.

Isabelle loves playing the harp because of its unique and essential voice in an orchestra. She covets for herself a parallel role in her family and in her circle of friends, but unfortunately, she usually feels marginal and dispensable. She compares her family to a troupe of actors, each obstinately rehearsing a part from a different play. While she loves and admires her father, he remains distant. She would have liked for "ce bel homme calme et mystérieux" to be her friend, but he seems unable to offer her anything more than spending money. She would like to relate to him more meaningfully than as "une grande fille muette et fausse" (63), but she never finds the right words. Having missed every opportunity, she laments, "Je suis seule. . . . Et tu es seul aussi" (89).

Isabelle identifies tacitly with her father; she even approves of his mistress, as she disparages her mother's excessive piety, fastidious housekeeping, and insipid tastes. Feeling especially lonely at one point, Isabelle considers confiding in her mother, but again, she lacks "la chose essentielle: le vocabulaire de la confiance" (62). Generally, Isabelle makes every effort not to think and act as her mother does. She renounces the Catholic faith and, later, declines to marry her perfectly respectable, devoted fiancé, explaining, "j'aurais trop peur de ressembler à ma mère et que tu ressembles à mon père" (163).

Isabelle chafes under the tyranny of her mother's possessive "affection maladive" (13), and she resents adult laughter and secrecy about subjects they say she is too young to understand. She does enjoy a visit with her aunt and uncle, however, because they treat her more or less as an adult and they allow her freedom "de tomber, de m'écorcher, de crier sans bouleverser l'order du monde" (14). She perceives her uncle as a sorcerer and respects him as a high priest when he allows her to participate in the quasi-ritual installation of an elaborate birdhouse he constructed. He teaches her the importance of undertaking creative projects for her own satisfaction: "c'est pour soi qu'on fait les choses, pour se donner à soi une réponse" (153). His role as philosopher and spiritual guide is similar to that of Tinamer's father in *L'Amélanchier*.

Isabelle attributes magical powers to her aunt, whose serenity she admires. Perhaps her aunt's bedtime stories of frightening adventures plant a subliminal message of hope in Isabelle's mind: help always comes when one needs it most.

Isabelle spends some of her summers as a little girl on a beautiful, secluded island near the home of another maternal uncle. In this natural setting, she explores her identity by forming a shape of herself in the sand. She relishes the sensations of the sun and wind. She states, "Je plongeais, exténuée, dans le ventre de la nature, les cheveux défaits, épars autour de moi comme mon âme" (20). Thoughts of the island sustain her through dreary winter months in the city. She plants imaginary birch trees, like the real ones growing on the island, to protect herself from unpleasant people and to mask the ugliness of her gray environment. The island, enhanced by transplanted memories of her aunt and her uncle Antoine's birdhouse, functions as Isabelle's personal mythological domain, providing her with a mental refuge as well as a sense of identity. She often retreats into the solitude of her inner self, where she deliberately cultivates a world that exists for her alone. There, as she phrases it, "j'imaginai de me séquestrer moi-même, au sein d'un univers fantastique où j'évoluais toute seule, libre, farouche et secrète" (10). It makes no difference that, some years later, Isabelle has not revisited the island, her aunt has died, and her uncle Antoine no longer recognizes her; her childhood domain remains intact.

As a young adult, Isabelle develops an intense, obsessive relationship with Stéphane, a disturbed man who introduces himself by evoking the exotic setting of his own Bohemian childhood. Isabelle loses her identity in his story as he rapes her in her practice room at the conservatory. She excuses his unpredictable violence, his lack of consideration, his alcoholism, and his theft of her money because she knows he suffered as a child and he still searches for the father who abandoned him. Hopelessly addicted to Stéphane, Isabelle lives for the moments when he treats her kindly. She finds herself imitating him, although she candidly equates her love for him with slavery. Once she tries to describe her island to Stéphane, but he mocks her. Jealously, he tries to destroy in her what is already dead in himself (57).

Isabelle barely contains her rage and disappointment when Julie, Stéphane's previously unacknowledged wife, returns unexpectedly to supplant her. Soon, however, Isabelle finds herself admiring and imitating Julie's actions and thinking her feminist thoughts. Recognizing Stéphane and Julie as "un vrai couple," Isabelle states, "je ne cherchais plus à les dissocier l'un de l'autre." She adds, "eux, ils étaient toute ma vie" (138). Isabelle fancies herself contributing some essential element to Stéphane's and Julie's relationship. To her chagrin, however, Stéphane and Julie eventually exclude her. They move away, abandoning her to a dreary, meaningless existence.

Reflecting on her alienation from herself, Isabelle describes her depression as a spiritual winter or a season in hell. Unable to take control of her life, she observes, "j'attendais encore du monde extérieur ma délivrance" (169). Bouthillette employs similar terms to describe Québec's dispossessed collective entity: "nous attendons toujours quelque chose dans notre long hiver intérieur" (52). Léger's assessment of Québec as "frappé d'une sorte d'impuissance à se déterminer" (349) applies also to Isabelle, as she vainly pursues truth and meaning outside of herself.

At her moment of deepest despair, Isabelle's childhood memories become her salvation. From the depths of her past, images of her summer island return to envelop her in her own dreams and her own personal truth (169). Spontaneously, she recalls the source of identity and purpose she had forgotten. She states, "seule, j'ai senti que je me dégageais du chaos," and drawing on the truth inherent in her childhood symbols, she triumphs over her personal darkness: "je me libérais peu à peu de mes esclavages" (171). Deciding to live her own life in her own way for once, she reiterates her uncle's admonition: "on ne joue pas pour un autre, on n'écrit pas pour un autre, on ne vit pas pour un autre" (153). With a new sense of dignity and self-esteem, Isabelle finds outlets for her stifled creativity: "je débouchais, une fois encore, sur l'infini, par la porte miraculeuse des poèmes" (171). By returning to her early sources of strength, Isabelle reestablishes her identity after a period of loss and confusion, much as Tinamer does in *L'Amélanchier*.

Cagnon remarks that since the 1960s many Québécois writers seem concerned with reversing Québec's "long ethnic death process." In their works, they explore the conflict between "a society's still possible death or its possible freedom and autonomy" (51). Ferron addresses this issue in *L'Amélanchier* through his portrayal of Tinamer, who takes her bearings by reminding herself of her origins, then proceeds confidently to pursue a career through which she may help others. As a revelatory dream enabled her to gain independence as a child, so recalling her childhood guides her out of her sense of futility and permits her to express herself freely and meaningfully as an adult. The legends and beliefs Tinamer acquired during her childhood symbolize Québec's rich cultural heritage. Ferron implies through his allegorical narrative that Québec should also take stock of the past, derive strength from the national identity thus affirmed, and then move forward confidently, socially and politically.

For *L'Ile joyeuse*, perhaps the more literary of the two works, a politically allegorical reading seems much less plausible. Maheux-Forcier states categorically that she does not write "pour livrer un message," or "pour témoigner de mon époque, de mon milieu, de mon pays." Instead, she writes "pour lutter contre la mort." She emphasizes, "JE DIS NON À LA MORT." While she defines her writing as being "de tous les temps et de partout" (Wyczynski 1971, 413–14), it is apparent that her personal struggle, as well as that of Isabelle in *L'Ile joyeuse*, may be considered in concert with concerns expressed by contemporary Québécois authors such as Ferron. Both Ferron and Maheux-Forcier guide their protagonists through a period of deep despondency that threatens their very existence. Through a process of remembering the magic and poetry of childhood, both Tinamer and Isabelle emerge vibrantly free, creative, and autonomous.

5

Refusal of the Adult World in Réjean Ducharme's *L'Océantume*

Réjean Ducharme, a novelist whose work has been described as "hautement charactéristique de la littérature québécoise actuelle" (Grandpré 1969, 4:173), develops childhood as a central theme. Ben-Zion Shek observes that Ducharme's characters engage in a "relentless battle" in order "to hold on to childhood and its fabulous and free contours" (1977, 293). In *L'Océantume* (1968), Iode, the ten-year-old protagonist, reports the episodes of her struggle against the adult world. Through her observations of her surroundings, her accounts of real and imaginary adventures and confessions of her deepest feelings, Ducharme creates, as Gilles Marcotte states it, "l'image de ce qui se passe, ici et maintenant" (1980, 72). In *L'Océantume*, Ducharme evokes and parodies some of the themes and images that typically appear in Québécois literature. He also explores some of the most complex aspects of Québec's collective consciousness.

L'Océantume, like many other Québécois novels published during the 1960s, calls for rejection of certain traditionally accepted values. From the first page of Ducharme's novel, rebellious Iode rejects and deliberately irritates the adults she encounters, especially her teacher. She disparages the "grosse valétudinaire" as a representative of absurd and obsolete authority. Like most adults, according to Iode, her teacher can be considered only subhuman: "elle fait partie d'une sorte d'interrègne mi-animal mi-autre chose" (20). Iode expresses her disdain by behaving in class "comme un glyptodon dans une glyptothèque" (22). Although she actually reads and writes very well, Iode feigns illiteracy because she would hate to give her teacher the satisfaction of thinking she had actually taught her something. Iode vehemently repulses her teacher's well-intentioned but clumsy efforts to interest her in school-work. Iode categorically rejects her along with the received values she transmits and the adult world she represents.

Iode causes a classmate to upset a religious statue and then reports with satisfaction, "Notre-Seigneur Jésus-Christ chancelle, penche, quitte son juchoir, s'écrase avec fracas" (115). In this manner, she dispenses with beliefs and practices she considers to be hollow, meaningless, and obsolete.

Iode's derision of her father connotes further rejection of traditional authority and of the status quo. An impractical dreamer, he spends all his time reading, smoking, and dozing beside a cold cup of tea. Iode remarks that he always seems content and that he never contradicts anyone. She under-scores his uselessness by describing him as her mother's "ex-fécondateur, son sperme passé" (33). He exercises absolute authority, however, in spite of his slackness. Renée Leduc-Park observes that his power "se révèle d'autant plus efficace qu'il est masqué par sa veulerie" (1982, 259). When Iode gets into trouble by abducting her neighbor's neglected cattle, her father promptly calls the police and sends her off to a deten-tion center for juvenile delinquents. Unexpectedly subju-gated to his "autorité ridicule," Iode contemptuously dismisses him as an actor who believes too much in his role (104). She refuses to love, respect, or accept "ce gnome gesticulant" as her father (83). By portraying him as irrele-vant, distant, and separate from her, by insisting on his lack of genuine concern for her well-being, and by protesting his arbitrary exercise of authority, Iode justifies her silent revolt. Iode's treatment of her father is humorous, expecially com-pared to the serious treatment of fathers in other Québécois novels of the 1960s, such as Marie-Claire Blais's *Manuscrits de Pauline Archange* and Claire Martin's *Dans un gant de fer*. Iode's father's behavior is nonetheless appalling. Her rebellion against him conveys the same collective rejection of traditional paternalistic power structures implied in other contemporary works.

Iode's dwelling, an abandoned steamship cemented lopsidedly beside a river and christened *Mange-de-la-merde* in defiance of public opinion, mocks the old family home around which childhood memories frequently converge in Québécois novels. Instead of revering the nostalgic "symbole collectif" identified by Denise Lemieux (1984, 22), Iode wishes her steamer would capsize. Nevertheless, the steamer fulfills the mythological function of "la vieille maison" as privileged center of childhood; Iode's dreams and adventures have their origin in its heart. Her deepest moments of reflection and self-awareness occur when she retreats into her own room in her family's unusual home. When Iode disparages the one place where she can truly be herself, her attitude approximates the feelings Pierre Vallières expresses toward his country in parts of *Nègres blancs d'Amérique*. At one point, having rejected his Québécois milieu, Vallières travels to France in search of happiness. Lonely and depressed, even contemplating suicide, he finally hears a friend's advice: "Tu as tort de tant mépriser ton pays. Il faut que tu apprennes à y vivre. . . . Aucun autre pays que le tien ne peut te donner ce que tu cherches" (264). Iode's comments about her home reflect the conflicting feelings of comfort and belonging, mixed with criticism and discontent, many Québécois experienced relative to their nation during the 1960s.

Ducharme draws some additional parallels between Québec and Iode's home in *L'Océantume*. A new family moves into a house across from the steamer near the beginning of the novel. Their little girl, Asie Azothe, naturally begins walking to school along the same road as Iode. Iode resents this intrusion, since she considers the road to be her own property. Indignant, she declares, "il est mon bien autant que ma chambre" (14). Therefore, comparing herself to French colonists who fired their cannons at English ships venturing into the Gulf of the Saint Lawrence, Iode throws pebbles at Asie Azothe and otherwise terrorizes her for trespassing. Further, since Iode's steamer sits on dry ground, it appears unnaturally static, reflecting a traditional nationalist insistance on the past. Cemented unevenly in place, it seems unstable, suggesting Québec's uncertain future from the perspective of the 1960s.

According to Lemieux, incest sometimes emerges as a leit-motiv in Québécois novels, especially those promulgating agriculturist ideology, because families are often portrayed as closed, isolated units (57). Further, Lemieux singles out Ducharme as an author whose work centers around themes of childhood and incest. She observes that he frequently depicts "la tendresse d'un couple fraternel se refusant à quitter l'en-fance, aliéné du monde" (53). While some Québécois novels may hint at uncomfortably close family relationships, Duch-arme treats incest blatantly and with humor in *L'Océantume* in particular. Iode and her brother Inachos, neglected by their parents and ostracized by the community because of their family's eccentricity, develop an unhealthy mutual depen-dency. Iode perceives herself and Inachos in mortal conflict with the rest of the world. She protects her weak, passive brother, declaring herself to be "sa vraie mère" (38). Insisting that no one else could ever understand or care for him as she does, she claims with irrational vehemence her right to be-come his wife and the mother of his children (47). When Asie Azothe expresses affection for Inachos, Iode attacks her rival with jealous fury. Excluded from the couple eventually formed by Inachos and Asie Azothe in spite of her wishes, Iode suffers terribly at the end of the novel. The other charac-ters evolve into conventional social roles, leaving Iode alone with her childhood concerns. By openly developing incest as a prominent theme and carrying it to a painful conclusion, Ducharme emphasizes the potentially tragic consequences of too much isolation and lack of healthy social exchange.

Ducharme also evokes in *L'Océantume* the mythological "north" or "elsewhere" identified by Jack Warwick as a prom-inent theme in Québécois literature in *L'Appel du nord dans la littérature canadienne-française.* Usually the exoticism of a distant land appeals to male characters, but in Ducharme's novel it is Iode's mother, Ina Ssouvie, as unfulfilled in life as her name suggests, who feels drawn to the distant unknown. When Ina abandons her family one spring, Iode identifies with her need to escape the banality of everyday existence: "J'aime comme une camarade cette Ina emportée par le retour des beaux jours" (104). Iode also expresses a desire to explore new territory when she exclaims restlessly, "que j'ai hâte d'être là où toute chose est nouvelle" (155). She and her brother spend their free time memorizing the names of obscure places they find in a gazeteer. They invent imaginary itineraries and adventures to entertain themselves and Asie Azothe. While most novelists merely allude to a distant mythical region and note its attraction for their protagonists, Ducharme permits Iode to actually pursue her dream of following the Atlantic shore "jusqu'à ce qu'il n'en reste plus" (55). Bored and despondent when Asie Azothe's parents send her away to a summer camp, Iode incites Inachos help her "rescue" their friend. The vicissitudes of their mission comprise the final sections of the novel and conclude when Iode and her companions finally arrive to find the ocean polluted and malodorous: "Il étend jusqu'à nos pieds une nappe transparente pleine de morceaux de poissons pourris qu'il ravale aussitôt" (190). Ducharme parodies the theme of the mythological "north" by demonstrating that the romantic notion of travel, and perhaps even the journey itself, may surpass the dubious pleasure of actually arriving at a destination.

Besides suggesting a comparison between his protagonist's personal territory and Québec, and besides providing unusual versions of some familiar themes in Québécois literature, Ducharme explores some complex and enigmatic aspects of Québec's collective consciousness in *L'Océantume.* Iode's ambivalent feelings toward her mother and toward Asie Asothe evoke the attitudes toward France and England that Jean Bouthillette attributes to Québec in his study *Le Canadien-français et son double.* Iode describes her birth as "difficile, douloureuse, impossible." Resisting the process, Iode "se débat sens dessus dessous" in her mother's womb, attempting to "grimper, remonter." Exasperated by Iode's lack of cooperation, and anxious to attend to her other children who were endangered by catastrophic, absurdly warlike events, Ina "attrape par un de ses pieds le foetus agité, l'arrache d'un coup de son ventre, l'emballe dans un drap et le laisse là" (35). Iode's description of her birth ressembles Bouthillette's discussion of Québec's break with France. He puts forth that the umbilical cord linking the colony to its mother country was severed brutally and too soon by "la Conquête." In his view, Québec was not ready to be "born"; it should have been given the opportunity to develop further as a colony and then later to obtain its independence from France, as the United States eventually became independent from Great Britain (1972, 24). Although Québec fought to remain part of France, it was, Bouthillette reiterates, abandoned by its uncaring mother (51). Historian Pierre Guillaume confirms the notion that France deliberately abandoned Québec when he states, "on ne peut que s'étonner que la France, dont les ressources humaines étaient tellement supérieures à celles de l'Angleterre . . . ait cédé aussi facilement le Canada à sa rivale." He concludes, "Il est évident qu'il n'y eut pas en France de volonté politique de garder le Canada," and further, "le Canada n'était donc toujours pas pour la France un enjeu important" (1984, 19–21). Thus, when Iode complains, "je suis née; j'ai les membres brisés" because she was violently rejected by her indifferent mother (35), she echos Bouthillette's observations about Québec: "notre naissance à nous-mêmes est non seulement prématurée, précaire et démunie, mais nos yeux s'ouvrent sur un monde hostile" (24).

Bouthillette maintains that Québec exhibits conflicting emotions in its attitudes toward France. Because the mother country abandoned its colonial offspring, Québec views France with equally irrational affection and resentment instead of treating it objectively as it would any other foreign country (51). Bouthillette believes that Québec developed "le complexe de l'abandonné" (52) as a result of being ceded to England. Iode's mixed feelings toward her mother reflect Québec's ambivalence toward France. On one hand, Iode repudiates her mother as a peevish, intemperate fanatic (57). If Iode's accounts of Ina's behavior are accurate, she certainly deserves reproof. In contrast to the traditional self-sacrificing mother of regionalist works, Ina drinks too much and ignores her family responsibilities. Frequently, when she has been drinking especially heavily, she embraces Iode, weeping and repeating, "Je suis ta maman." Iode resigns herself to enduring these sentimental scenes, but she prefers to believe that she actually brought herself into the world (22). On the other hand, Iode behaves badly in order to attract her mother's attention, or so her social worker claims (85). She steals potatoes from fields on her way to school and wipes the dirt on the front of the dress she claims to have been wearing daily for three years. Picking lice provides her with a welcome distraction during boring lessons. Iode seems to enjoy cultivating a deliberately annoying personality. She admits to dropping her false identity in order to become her true self, equally repulsive, alone in her room at night.

In Bouthillette's view, Québec resembles an orphan returning "au pays de l'enfance pour mieux retrouver une mère perdue ou la mieux flétrir" (52). Further, as a result of its abandonment, he affirms that Québec entered into an "isolement intérieur" that only became deeper with time (51). Iode also isolates herself, stifling her emotions inside a hard, protective shell: "Je suis au centre d'un bloc de pierre!" (21). Alone in her room, Iode excludes the outside world, exclaiming, "Que je reste à l'abri au fond de moi-même! Que je me garde intacte, entière" (21). Her attitude can be seen as reflecting Québec's cultural isolation following "la Conquête."

Some aspects of Iode's friendship with Asie Azothe mirror the relationship between the Québec and England, as illuminated by Bouthillette. Initially Iode defends her territory against Asie Azothe's intrusion, comparing herself to the

French colonists who fired their cannons at English invaders. Iode hints at a further association of Asie Azothe with England when she uses English words to express her jealous admiration: "ses doigts sont si *small*, si *little*" (19). Overcome by feelings of inferiority inspired by beautiful, sweet, conscientious Asie Azothe, Iode confirms Bouthillette's observation that the English language "est devenue synonyme de progrès et de réussite" (44). Bouthillette affirms that, faced with English economic success, Québec seems isolated and powerless (41). Similarly, confronted by Asie Azothe's obvious social and academic superiority, Iode remarks, "mon impuissance m'impatiente" (15).

Perhaps seduced by the exotic appeal of her name or the all-pervasive quality it implies (*azote* translates as "nitrogen"), Iode soon yields to Asie Azothe's charm: "je me sens vaincue et je me laisse entraîner de désir et de curiosité" (17). Iode gradually absorbs her friend's personality into her own to the point that they seem to become the same person (81). Sometimes Iode has the sensation of actually wearing the same dress as Asie Azothe, having her same blond hair and thinking her thoughts (117). Renée Leduc-Park suggests that Iode goes so far as to attempt to merge her own personality with her friend's in order to make herself more attractive to her brother, who clearly prefers Asie Azothe (226). Bouthillette asserts that a similar collective transformation occurs when the Québécois are forced to use English for business purposes. He declares that, because of contemporary socioeconomic structures, Québec must adopt a "visage anglais" (40). By developing the habit of viewing themselves from an English perspective, the Québécois become to some degree English, which results in an abnormal doubling of their own personality (48). This assimilation is dangerous in Bouthillette's view because it implies a proportionate loss of Québécois identity. Iode resists the loss of her own personality by instinctively repulsing her friend: "Asie Azothe, rose parlante, je te vomis de ma vie" (53). Iode's rejection of Asie Azothe, upon whom

she inevitably depends, clearly illustrates one aspect of Bouthillette's analysis of Québec's complex relationship to English Canada.

Bouthillette claims that deep feelings of powerlessness
penetrate Québec (91). Unable to take action, Québec merely
reacts defensively to decisions made by others: "le monde se
fait sans nous et nous agissons à son encontre" (52). Iode
approaches life in much the same manner in *L'Océantume*.
Painfully aware of her insignificance, she complains, "je n'ai
autorité sur rien. Rien ne changera par moi" (154). Incapable
of influencing her world, she carefully cultivates an attitude of
detached indifference (25). Reality ultimately penetrates her
defense and forces her to acknowledge feelings of horror,
disgust, and pain (24).

Iode alleviates her suffering to some extent by creating a
fantasy world in which she alone reigns. She replaces her
banal existence with vibrant adventures of her own invention.
Bouthillette observes that Québec similarly countered feelings of powerlessness by creating an identity based on myth
and by existing in imaginary "terres idylliques" (56). In his
view, this retreat from reality indicates a subconscious refusal
of "la Conquête" and an unwillingness to acknowledge the
subsequent centuries of English presence (53).

As head of her own autocracy, Iode silently declares war on
the rest of the world (186). In her experience, the world
seems pleasant only as long as she allows herself to be domi-
nated by others. As soon as she stops accepting a subordinate
role, she discovers the truly oppressive nature of "la Milliarde," the adult collectivity against which she militates. Her
battle is a matter of life and death, she explains; one must
conquer or be conquered (51). Iode's ruthless "Milliarde"
could be compared to the English political and economic
power structure Bouthillette perceives as a formidable enemy.
He asserts that it unconsciously exploits the people of Québec
and strips them to the bone (57). Iode refuses to contribute to
the system by allowing herself to be its victim. Iode's bellig-

erence echos Paul Emile Borduas's *Refus global:* "Rompre définitivement avec toutes les habitudes de la société, se désolidariser de son esprit utilitaire" (1978, 50).

When Iode compares her mortal enemy to the ocean, she acknowledges the futility of her struggle: "Plus il y a d'eau, plus l'océan est grand. Plus il y a d'ennemis, moins la victoire est possible" (52). Her analogy explains her growing apprehension as she travels inexorably toward the Atlantic coast in the company of her mother and her social worker, both confirmed members of "la Milliarde." Caught between the two adults, the wind blowing their hair against her face, Iode finds herself inextricably associated with them. Despair overwhelms Iode as their shadows darken the sand. She approaches the stinking ocean "ayant la certitude de marcher vers ma perte" (190). Iode's ultimate absorption into the ranks of "la Milliarde" is suggested by André Vanasse's interpretation of the novel's title as "l'océan t'hume" (1977, 23), that is, the ocean inhales you or takes you in. That she should be sucked into "la Milliarde" seems inevitable in spite of her admirable resistance. She resigns herself to accepting the putrefaction of adult reality, declaring "Nous y sommes. Soyons-y!" (190).

Perhaps Iode was always integrally associated with the ocean by virtue of her name ("iodine"). When she protests the presence of adults, wondering "qui les a laissées s'introduire dans nos secrets d'enfants" (190), she seems to forget that she was actually the one who invited them. While some critics question Iode's sincerity as a narrator at this point (Leduc-Park 1982, 192–93), a plausible explanation for her apparent contradictions can be found in Bouthillette, who posits an unconscious collaboration on the part of the Québécois in the very system that destroys their identity. His thesis is that the Québécois have internalized an English perspective of themselves. Consequently, they have assimilated a double personality at war with itself. The English side convinces them of the English system's progressiveness. Since a system perceived as fair and reasonable must obviously be accepted, Québec risks self-annihilation in order to adopt the only apparently rational option: cooperation and resignation (60).

Many different interpretations of *L'Océantume* may be proposed, since the essence of Ducharme's text is "la mise en valeur des innombrables possibilités du signifiant" (Vanasse 1977, 23). Lemieux asserts that Ducharme's emphasis on childhood constitutes "une recherche de la patrie" (55). Shek sees "the quest for a satisfying self-image" in Iode's obstinate refusal of the adult world (293). It would be erroneous and reductive, however, to treat Iode as a variation on Peter Pan's refusal to grow up. It is important to recognize Iode's rejection of the adult world as a repudiation of the depersonalizing political and economic system it represents.

L'Océantume expresses the same desire to eradicate traditional patterns of authority and meaningless, repressive religious practices as may be read in many contemporary works. Certain leitmotivs common in Québécois literature weave through Ducharme's text, sometimes with an unusual twist. More importantly, however, *L'Océantume* explores some complex aspects of Québec's collective personality. References to Bouthillette's analysis illuminate Iode's ambivalent attitude toward her mother as an allusion to Québec's view of France as a loved and hated "mère patrie." Iode's friendship with Asie Azothe reveals Québec's insidious, identity-threatening tendency to assimilate the English personality. Finally, Bouthillette's argument that Québec's oppressive, English-dominated socioeconomic system appears to be just and reasonable, even though it implies total Québécois effacement, sheds light on Iode's eventual capitulation to the forces she had so valiantly resisted. Iode personifies Québec to the extent that her behavior in *L'Océantume* reflects the collective mentality. While Ducharme ironically abandons his protagonist to her doom, Bouthillette expresses more optimism for Québec. He declares, "notre libération . . . voit enfin poindre le jour" (96).

6

A Comparison of Childhood in Selected English-Canadian and Québécois Novels

In *Everyday Magic: Child Languages in Canadian Literature*, Laurie Ricou analyzes the ways in which children's perspectives have been interpreted in writing. Although he limits his study to Canadian literature written in English, he comments in a bibliographical note on the pervasiveness of child imagery, suggesting that "literature written in French in Canada is perhaps even more attached to the child figure than literature in English" (1987, 140).

Ricou observes that "a study of the image of childhood in Canadian literature could be massive" (139). A comparative analysis of the treatment of childhood in Québécois and in English-Canadian literature could be equally large. Ronald Sutherland is one of few critics to approach such a comparison; he devotes a section of *Second Image* to childhood in Réjean Ducharme's *L'Avalée des avalés* (1966) and in W. O. Mitchell's *Who Has Seen the Wind* (1947). As a contribution to the potentially massive, potentially illuminating, and potentially non-conclusive body of comparative studies of English-Canadian and Québécois literature, I would like to propose a discussion of childhood in *Raisins and Almonds* (1972), a Jewish-Canadian autobiographical novel by Fredelle Bruser Maynard, along with a comparison between Gabrielle Roy's *Rue Deschambault* (1955) and Alice Munro's *Lives of Girls and Women* (1971).

In *Raisins and Almonds*, Maynard treats childhood in a manner similar to autobiographical novels by Québécois authors Philippe Aubert de Gaspé and Robert de Roquebrune. Like the Québécois authors, Maynard writes about her childhood in order to safeguard the memory of a unique time and place. She begins *Raisins and Almonds* by evoking the natural beauty of her childhood home, adding "it can never come again, that free wild perilous world" (13). Similar emotions reverberate from passages of *Mémoires*, where Gaspé laments, "Que les temps sont changés depuis ma jeunesse" (20), and from *Testament de mon enfance*, where Roquebrune compares the "éternité heureuse" of his childhood with the present: "Rien ne ressemble plus à ce qu'était alors l'existence" (11). Maynard recalls her early childhood games and pastimes in much the same terms as Gaspé and Roquebrune use. Her family's home surrounds her with an atmosphere of "gentility and comfort" (22), comparable to that of the old Québécois manor houses. Like Gaspé and Roquebrune, who recall nostalgically the natural setting of their youthful experiences, Maynard remembers "the dusky lavender light" of blissful evenings in Birch Hills: "we have gathered in the field by the skating rink; the town lies behind us, the woods thicken rough. I smell crushed grass and clover" (26). Margaret Martinello classifies Maynard's work, along with Gaspé's *Mémoires* and Roquebrune's *Testament de mon enfance*, as "pastoral" (1980, 217).

While the essence of Gaspé's and Roquebrune's writing is the preservation of memory, Maynard alludes to some additional, more compelling motivations for her work. As Martinello observes, since some of Maynard's memories are "troublesome," her autobiography "also functions as a confession" and as an opportunity "to correct the imbalance" of her earlier rejection of her Jewish faith (213). As an adult, having lost her bearings, like Tinamer de Portanqueu in Jacques Ferron's *L'Amélanchier*, Maynard returns to her sources "to understand" and to answer the urgent question, "who am I?" (181).

Maynard seeks her identity in her Jewish heritage, which,

as a child, she found to be more of a burden than a source of strength. She confides, "reluctant conscript to a doomed army, I longed to change sides" (29). Her cultural distinction conflicts painfully with her obsessive desire to fit in with her peers. She affirms, "difference was in my bones and blood, and in the pattern of my separate life" (27). Growing up in a community of sturdy Scandinavian farmers, Maynard critically observes her own rather intellectual shopkeeper father: "I was proud of his good looks, and yet uneasy about their distinctly oriental flavor" (27). No less beautiful, Maynard's short, heavy-set mother differs strikingly from her slim, blond, blue-eyed neighbors. Describing her grandfather, with "a black cap and a long beard bent over the Talmud," as "unreal," she recalls, "I felt for him a kind of amused tenderness, but I was glad that my schoolmates could not see him" (28).

Maynard's parents seem comfortable with their differences; they participate graciously in community activities while their daughter struggles painfully, trapped between two cultures.

Gaspé and Roquebrune remember playing tranquilly alone or with their siblings. Maynard, in contrast, worries constantly that her friends might exclude her from their plans. She orders a special lotion from Eaton's to make her skin light like her friend Fern's. Always insecure, she suffers through intol-erably long Sundays, forced to entertain herself alone while Fern and the others attend church. Her happiest memories are of other children calling her name, drawing her into their evening game of Red Rover (26).

As in the novels by Gaspé and Roquebrune, a move to the city signals an end to Maynard's early childhood happiness. As children, Gaspé and Roquebrune, whose families moved to enhance their father's careers, welcomed the opportunity to explore new surroundings. Maynard, however, realizing that her father's business failed, experiences sadness and despair. Before leaving, she instinctively, and with a sense of futility, inscribes her identity on the Saskatchewan prairie: "I lifted my foot and, heel to toe, stamped out my name in the snow" (65). Maynard's optimism about "belonging" in her new home in Winnipeg fades when she discovers that her father's new store is located in "alien territory" instead of in a Jewish neighborhood (71). Her disappointment intensifies the ugliness of the urban environment and the humiliations she suffers at school.

In her article, "The Uncertain Countries of Jacques Ferron and Mordecai Richler," Eileen Sarkar identifies some thematic similarities in literature produced by members of minority groups in Canada. She notes that "the French Canadians of Quebec and the Jewish inhabitants of the Montreal ghetto both feel their continued existence threatened" (1974, 98). For this reason, she posits, writers representing both groups "articulate the existence" of their respective cultures and attempt to "prove the worth of that existence" (102). Sarkar's observations certainly apply to *Raisins and Almonds*, in which Maynard goes to great lengths to portray her family life and her Jewish heritage in a positive light. Both Roquebrune and Gaspé also bear witness to Québec's rich cultural heritage as they preserve their personal recollections.

Jean-Charles Falardeau remarks that solitude and alienation recur as dominant themes in both Jewish-Canadian and Québécois literature (1972, 60–61). Maynard indeed portrays her child self as profoundly alone, separated from her companions by the glass wall of her ethnicity. The warm, nurturing, and supportive environment provided by her parents fails to mitigate her intense and frustrated desire for total acceptance by her friends. Gaspé and Roquebrune, in the comparable retrospective Québécois treatments of childhood, also express solitude and alienation, but in a different way. As they perceived themselves as children, Gaspé and Roquebrune were sometimes alone, but they were not lonely. As adults, however, they experience solitude because many of their childhood companions have passed away. Alienated from their idealized past, almost as if they had been expelled from paradise, they view themselves as anachronisms. Tinamer in Ferron's *L'Amélanchier* also expresses a sense of loss and estrangement as an adult, although as a child she felt fully secure at home and fully accepted by her cheerful school-mates. Ducharme's child protagonist in *L'Océantume* experiences isolation, but she approaches her situation entirely differently from Maynard. Instead of denying her identity in order to resemble other children more closely, she deliberately emphasizes her difference. She sets herself up as the standard and systematically rejects those who disapprove of her behavior.

In general, Québécois authors focus on their child protagonists individually and in the context of their family relationships; they rarely dwell on the nature of the children's social interactions. The children seem to form friendships easily and naturally, without attaching undue significance to them. Most of the protagonists allude to their childhood companions collectively, without mentioning their names; Isabelle in *L'Île joyeuse,* for example, recalls only "quelques beaux visages" from among her childhood companions (24), while Tinamer evokes her "joyeuses amies" collectively, in passing, in *L'Amélanchier* (111). Iode goes so far as to resent the presence of her devoted friend in *L'Océantume.* She exclaims: "J'ai hâte que Asie Azothe meure pour être seule" (105).

Obviously, children like Maynard, singled out as the only Jewish child in her school, would exhibit a stronger need for approval and acceptance than children who belong to their community's ethnic majority. Sociologists Alan Anderson and James Frideres consider the Québécois to be "a very cohesive group" because of their "common heritage derived from French history" and their "longstanding variety of French culture developed during three and a half centuries of residence in Canada" (1981, 86). Since Québec's class structure is relatively rigid, according to John Porter's well-known study of social class and power, *The Vertical Mosaic* (1967, 93), the absence of struggles for status portrayed among children in Québécois literature would reflect the security inherent in belonging to a clearly identified majority group along with the stability implied by that group's stratified social structure.

In his analysis of childhood autobiographies, Richard Coe puts forth that the English-Canadian child "appears fascinated over and over again, not by its own past self, but rather that self's relation to the community" (1984, 279). Coe's observation is borne out in works such as Alice Munro's *Lives of Girls and Women*, Sylvia Fraser's *Pandora* (1972), and Ernest Buckler's *The Mountain and the Valley* (1952), as well as in Maynard's *Raisins and Almonds*.

In *Lives of Girls and Women*, Munro's protagonist, Del Jordan, explains that three distinct social groups comprise her class. Certain students, by virtue of their parents' influence in the community, always become the hall monitors and Junior Red Cross representatives or the star in the school play. Teachers inevitably assign them these coveted roles, or as Del attests, "we unhesitatingly and with a graceful sense of what was fitting, elected them ourselves" (122). Del places the misfits on the opposite end of the classroom social hierarchy. In between, Del joins the ranks of "the ambitious and unsure," who hope desperately for even a minor role in the school operetta. Certain that exclusion from the performance would devastate her already shaky social status, Del exclaims, "I could not believe in injustice so terrible as to keep me off that stage" (124).

Although students in Fraser's *Pandora* appear to be "an accidental assortment of carefree girls who like to skip," they are in fact "a jostling selection of anxious girls in the process of forming a society" (81). Having learned from her earlier mistakes in social strategy, Pandora swiftly accomplishes her "primary goal" on the first day of second grade by obtaining "a prestige seat in the smartness hierarchy, surrounded by as many as possible of her bestfriends" (145). Pandora shrewdly selects a popular companion who will enhance her own status as well as spare her the humiliation of "being paired, forcibly, by the teacher with another 'leftover'" (149).

Buckler's protagonist, David Canaan, allows peer pressure to spoil his childhood happiness in *The Mountain and the Valley*. At the end of a school play, still caught up in his princely role,

David impulsively kisses the princess, his childhood sweetheart, Effie. The mocking laughter of older boys, whose critical presence he had not noticed previously, makes him feel ridiculous. Suddenly the magic disappears, leaving only "the raw edges of the flimsy cardboard and the verdigris on the clasp weldings of Effie's rhinestone brooch" (82). Angry and ashamed, David stumbles into adult reality. His self-conscious concern for the older boys' approval expels him from the promised land of childhood innocence his name suggests.

Maynard's concern with her social status obviously reflects the struggles of an immigrant ethnic minority attempting to assimilate the dominant English-Canadian culture. For reasons that may be explained in part by Porter's analysis of Canadian class structure (the complexity of which exceeds the scope of this study), children who already belong to the English-speaking majority strive nonetheless to establish for themselves a favorable position within the group. While Maynard's evocation of solitude and her emphasis on valorizing her ethnic affiliation liken her work to Québécois treatments of childhood, her obsession with social acceptance links her account of childhood more closely to English-Canadian works.

In his comparison of Margaret Laurence's *A Bird in the House* (1970) with Alice Munro's *Lives of Girls and Women*, Ricou suggests that the two authors seek "an alternative to the Bildungsroman," typically a male genre, by fictionalizing their childhood experiences in a serial format and by including some feminist themes (23). If he had envisioned treating Canadian literature written in French as part of his study, he might have considered including Gabrielle Roy's *Rue Deschambault* in this chapter. Roy's work, like Munro's and Laurence's, is structured as a series of related, self-contained, roughly chronological short stories in which an adult writer narrates her recollections of childhood and adolescence. Ricou observes that the theme of "heredity" linking "the lives of girls, adolescents and women" figures prominently in the

English-Canadian works (16), and that, in Munro's work especially, "the girl's search for a relationship with her mother" constitutes "an important narrative element" (24). Paula Gilbert Lewis observes, in her comprehensive study of Gabrielle Roy's literary vision, that Christine, the narrator of *Rue Deschambault*, "clearly exhibits the power of inheritance" (1984, 34). Lewis comments on the powerful influence of mothers in Roy's fiction and remarks that intimate mother-daughter relationships "are always realistically described" (35). In spite of differences in the cultural and social environments in which the two works are set, striking similarities exist in the rapport between mothers and daughters in Munro's *Lives of Girls and Women* and in Roy's *Rue Deschambault*.

While fathers are absent—in *Lives of Girls and Women*, hunting occupies Del's father, and in *Rue Deschambault*, Christine's morose father travels on business—the young women learn from their mothers' lives. Both mothers test the limits of their traditional roles by undertaking ambitious projects unusual for women of their time. Christine's mother fulfills a dream by taking the train across Canada to visit relatives in Québec. Before departing, she earns money by sewing, finds temporary homes for her children, and leaves a note for her husband who, if he had been consulted, would certainly have forbidden the journey. Del's mother gains some independence by learning to drive, to the consternation of Del's maiden aunts, and by selling encyclopedias. She expresses her unconventional views in occasional speeches and letters to the local newspaper.

Both Christine and Del sense their mothers' vague dissatisfaction with their lives. Christine recalls that "Maman, dans le passé, avait déjà parlé d'être libre" (99). Although "Maman" affirms her love for her home and family, Christine understands that her responsibilities prevented her from accomplishing or experiencing anything extraordinary. Del, who once thought of her mother as a priestess, supposing her "powerful, a ruler, also content," later finds her rather ordinary, "just my mother in Jubilee" (79). Del observes sympathetically that her mother's intellectual needs go unmet in Jubilee.

Assessing their mothers' situations critically, both Del and Christine aspire to a different, richer life. Their mothers actively encourage them to leave home, pursue an education, and experience life as fully as possible. When Del becomes "distracted" from her studies by a boyfriend, her mother scolds, "Do you intend to live in Jubilee all your life? Do you want to be the wife of a lumberyard worker? Do you want to join the Baptist Ladies Aid?" (217). Del resists her mother's admonitions as a matter of form: "Her concern about my life, which I needed and took for granted, I could not bear to have expressed" (173), but she does eventually leave Jubilee to pursue her career as a writer. Although Christine's mother taught her "le pouvoir des images, la merveille d'une chose révélée par un mot juste et tout l'amour que peut contenir une simple et belle phrase" (246), she seems surprised when Christine announces her plans to become a writer. Insightfully pointing out some potential difficulties, she suggests that Christine also prepare to teach. Christine sighs, "Maman avait souhaité faire de toutes ses filles des maîtresses d'école—peut-être parce qu'elle portait en elle-même, parmi tant de rêves sacrifiés, cette vocation manquée" (283); lacking more specific plans, however, she complies.

Delores Gros-Louis notes that mothers in English-Canadian works such as Laurence's *A Bird in the House* and Audrey Thomas's *Songs My Mother Taught Me* (1973), as well as in Munro's *Lives of Girls and Women*, foster their daughters' independence (1976–77, 9–10). In contrast, mothers in Québécois novels resign themselves to their restricted role in life without envisioning a different future for their daughters. Neither Tinamer's mother in *L'Amélanchier*, who prepares her meals "l'air de dire: quand ce n'est pas un repas, c'est un autre" (88), nor Isabelle's mother, who "se définissait par le nettoyage" in *L'Ile joyeuse* (61), offers guidance or encouragement, although Tinamer and Isabelle both benefit from their negative example. Roy's work certainly stands out from a feminist perspective, considering that it predates most of the other novels mentioned by more than ten years. Roy's treatment of Christine's relationship to her mother establishes a strong thematic link between her work and Munro's *Lives of Girls and Women*, as well as with certain other recent English-Canadian novels.

In other areas, particularly in the treatment of friendships, *Rue Deschambault* aligns itself more closely with Québécois works. Roy's protagonist, Christine, lives in Winnipeg, like Maynard in *Raisins and Almonds*, except that Christine grows up in the French-speaking section, Saint-Boniface. In an article assessing her Manitoba heritage, Roy alludes to the fervor of French culture in this francophone enclave: "Saint-Boniface, alors, respirait, priait, espérait, chantait, souffrait, on pourrait dire, en français, gagnant cependant son pain en anglais, dans les bureaux, les magasins et les usines de Winnipeg." She further remarks that, crossing the river into the main, anglophone part of the city, "nous entrions dans un autre monde" (1970, 75). In *Rue Deschambault*, Christine never expresses a desire to be part of this "other world." Surrounded by French-speaking families like her own, immersed in her own culture, Christine clearly has the sense of belonging that Maynard, as an isolated member of her ethnic minority, always misses. Accordingly, Roy treats Christine's childhood friendships in much the same manner as Blais, Ferron, Maheux-Forcier, and Ducharme do; their protagonists choose companions within their Québécois community easily and without regard for their social status. Roy mentions Christine's friends in passing when illness confines her to her bed and she misses them, but the focus is clearly on Christine, who soon learns to prefer her solitary reveries. She wonders, "comment ne sait-on pas plus tôt qu'on est soi-même son meilleur, son plus cher compagnon?" (84).

Ronald Sutherland devotes a section of *Second Image*, a comparative study of Canadian literature, to the treatment of childhood. He bases his discussion on Réjean Ducharme's

L'Avalée des avalés and W. O. Mitchell's *Who Has Seen the Wind*. His conclusion that the two works have similar "thematic and technical qualities" and that they both present "non-idealistic, even cynical" child protagonists (1971, 106) supports his initial hypothesis that "when French-Canadian and English-Canadian novels are examined together, it becomes evident that . . . a good number of the accepted differences between the cultures of French Canada and English Canada do not in fact exist" (3).

Comparisons of other treatments of childhood in Canada reveal other similarities as well as differences. If childhood is considered in terms of self-discovery and establishing identity, a marked difference may be noted between children in English-Canadian novels, who tend to define themselves in relation to others, and children in Québécois novels, who seek their identity individually and in the context of their cultural heritage.

This disparity points to the ongoing debate between "diversité ethnique" and "unité nationale" so prevalent in Canadian politics. Jean-Michel Lacroix remarks in his discussion of this complex issue that "le discours idéologique tourne autour de la question de l'assimilation ou du pluralisme" (1984, 189). Maynard's dilemma in *Raisins and Almonds*, in which her ethnicity impedes the social acceptance she so ardently desires, reflects the national preoccupation Lacroix acknowledges. Maynard expresses an immigrant's hopeful aspirations in her youthful eagerness to merge with the dominant culture. Her subsequent return to childhood in search of her repressed identity attests to the psychic loss inherent in assimilation.

Passages in *Lives of Girls and Women* illustrate struggles within the controlling socioeconomic hierarchy: children of the elite automatically succeed at school, while middle-class children like Del attempt to improve their status over the socially inadept.

In comparable Québécois novels, children rarely, if ever, attempt to repress or efface their ethnic identity even though, as Porter affirms, it implies limited socioeconomic mobility

(73). Some children attempt to improve the quality of their life through eduction, as in Marie-Claire Blais's *Manuscrits de Pauline Archange*, but their ambitions are not portrayed as extending beyond their ethnic sector. Their efforts to establish or reestablish identity by remembering the past and by renewing their faith in personal legends and beliefs put them in touch again with Québec's historical and cultural sources of strength and unity. The Québécois novelists appear to advocate assertion of national identity as preferable to achieving economic success.

To the extent that anglophone culture controls the possibilities of individual economic advancement, materialism actually outweighs nationalist sentiment in Québec, Louis Balthazar has observed (1989, 121). In 1987 the Meech Lake Accord officially acknowledged the duality of Canada. In spite of this unprecedented constitutional recognition of Québec's specificity, a breaking down of what Porter designates as "the ethnic impediment to equality, particularly the equality of opportunity" (73) must occur in order for Québec's distinct society to thrive.

7
Conclusion

Childhood recurs continually as a theme in Québécois novels, as well as in theater and poetry. Emphasizing this fact, M. L. Piccione observes that "la liste serait longue de tous les personnages romanesques ou dramatiques qui se 'raccrochent' à leur passé" (1984, 264), while Lucille Roy-Hewitson attests that Québec's most prominent poets "en ont fait le centre de leur oeuvre, une source d'inspiration constante" (1980, 35). Most of the novels that treat childhood extensively fall roughly into three categories.

On one hand, in novels intended to criticize corruption in society, innocent child protagonists provide an effective narrative strategy. Marie-Claire Blais employs this technique to advantage in *Manuscrits de Pauline Archange* and in some of her other earlier works. Réjean Ducharme mocks social conventions by adopting the viewpoint of his rebellious youthful narrator in *L'Océantume*. Jacques Poulin's endearing child protagonist watches his home disintegrate literally and figuratively in *Jimmy* (1969). The child as victim and social observer figures prominently in novels published in Québec during the 1960s.

On the other hand, a number of novels may be seen as expressions of the "roots phenomenon," a general effort mobilized in the late 1960s and early 1970s to valorize ethnic and cultural differences (Lacroix 1984, 219). Louise Maheux-Forcier's Isabelle in *L'Ile joyeuse* and Jacques Ferron's Tinamer in *L'Amélanchier* offer examples of adult narrators who return to their sources in search of strength, direction, and purpose. A more recent variation on this theme may be found in Anne Hébert's *Le Premier jardin* (1988), in which the protagonist feels compelled to return to Québec in order to relive cathartically a tragic event from her childhood.

Fictionalized autobiographies comprise the largest category of Québécois novels treating childhood. Some of these works, such as Philippe Aubert de Gaspé's *Mémoires,* Laure Conan's *Angéline de Montbrun,* and Robert de Roquebrune's *Testament de mon enfance* portray the past in poignantly nostalgic terms. A deep sense of loss pervades these accounts of "paradis perdu." Other authors, such as Roch Carrier, dwell with tender amusement on the adventures of their former selves. Authors of semiautobiographical novels seem particularly concerned with memory and writing, since, as Richard Coe maintains, the inevitable conflict between the author's commitment to honesty and to creating readable literature must be acknowledged and resolved (1984, 86–87). Gabrielle Roy addresses these issues in *Rue Deschambault;* André Brochu also discusses them in his autobiographical passages devoted to childhood in *La Visée critique* (1988).

One theme, perhaps the strongest, that consistently pervades novels of childhood is that of establishing identity. While this statement could be applied cross-culturally and universally, it can be argued that Québécois authors treat the question of identity with particular urgency. In view of continuing tensions between Canada's two main linguistic groups (Gagnon and Montcalm 1990, 190), and in view of declining birth rates, economic factors that favor migration away from the francophone province, and the increasing influx of immigrants (Massé 1989, 111), maintenance of Québec's distinct and unique national identity becomes, perhaps more than ever, a vital issue. Since childhood affords a propitious pretext for exploring questions of identity, this theme is likely to persist in the literature of Québec.

References

Anderson, Alan B., and James S. Frideres. *Ethnicity in Canada.* Toronto: Butterworths, 1981.

Ariès, Philippe. *Centuries of Childhood,* trans. Robert Baldick. New York: Knopf, 1962.

Atwood, Margaret. "Un Petit rat heureux." *Le Magazine Maclean* 15.9 (1975): 19–21, 43.

Balthazar, Louis. "Nationalism in Québec: Past, Present, and Future." *Québec Studies* 8 (1989): 120–23.

Blais, Marie-Claire. *La Belle bête.* Québec: Institut Littéraire du Québec, 1959.

———. *L'Exécution.* Montréal: Editions du Jour, 1968.

———. *Manuscrits de Pauline Archange.* Montréal: Editions du Jour, 1968.

———. *Une Saison dans la vie d'Emmanuel.* 1966. Reprint. Montréal: Stanké, 1980.

———. *Tête blanche.* Québec: Institut Littéraire du Québec, 1960.

Blodgett, E. D. "The Father's Seduction: The Example of Laure Conan's *Angéline de Montbrun.*" In *A Mazing Space,* ed. Shirley Neuman and Smaro Kamboureli. Edmonton: Longspoon, 1986.

Borduas, Paul Emile. *Ecrits/Writings, 1942–1958,* ed. François-Marc Gagnon. New York: New York University Press, 1978.

Boucher, Jean-Pierre. *Jacques Ferron au pays des amélanchiers.* Montréal: Presses de l'Université de Montréal, 1973.

Bouthillette, Jean. *Le Canadien-français et son double.* Ottawa: Hexagone, 1972.

Boynard-Frot, Janine. "Une lecture féministe des romans du terroir canadien-français de 1860 à 1960." *Possibles* 4 (1979): 41–53.

Brochu, André. *La Visée critique.* Montréal: Boréal, 1988.

Buckler, Ernest. *The Mountain and the Valley.* 1952. Reprint. Toronto: McClelland and Stewart, 1961.

Cagnon, Maurice. *The French Novel of Québec.* Boston: Twayne, 1986.

Carrier, Roch. *Les Enfants du bonhomme dans la lune.* 1979. Reprint. Montréal: Stanké, 1983.

Chatillon, Pierre. "Les Thèmes de l'enfance et de la mort dans l'oeuvre poétique de Nelligan, Saint-Denys-Garneau, Anne Hébert et Alain Grandbois." Ph.D. diss., Université de Montréal, 1961.

Coe, Richard N. *When the Grass Was Taller*. New Haven, Conn.: Yale University Press, 1984.

Conan, Laure. *Angéline de Montbrun*. 1884. Reprint. Montréal: Fides, 1980.

Ducharme, Réjean. *L'Avalée des avalés*. Paris: Gallimard, 1966.

———. *L'Océantume*. Paris: Gallimard, 1968.

Ducrocq-Poirier, Madeleine. *Le Roman canadien de lanque française de 1860 à 1958*. Paris: Nizet, 1978.

Dumont, Micheline, and Nadia Fahmy-Eid. *Les Couventines*. Montréal: Boréal, 1986.

Falardeau, Jean-Charles. *Notre société et son roman*. Montréal: HMH, 1972.

Ferron, Jacques. *L'Amélanchier*. Montréal: VLB Editeur, 1970.

———. *The Juneberry Tree (L'Amélanchier)*, trans. Raymond Chamberlain. Montréal: Harvest House, 1975.

Fraser, Sylvia. *Pandora*. Toronto: McClelland and Stewart, 1972.

Gagnon, Alain, and Mary Beth Montcalm. *Quebec: Beyond the Quiet Revolution*. Scarborough, Ont.: Nelson Canada, 1990.

Gallays, François. "Reflections in the Pool: The Subtext of Laure Conan's *Angéline de Montbrun*." In *Traditionalism, Nationalism, and Feminism*, ed. Paula Gilbert Lewis. Westport, Conn.: Greenwood, 1985.

Gaspé, Philippe Aubert de (fils). *Le Chercheur de Trésors; ou, L'Influence d'un livre*. 1837. Reprint. Montréal: Réedition-Québec, 1969.

Gaspé, Philippe Aubert de (père). *Mémoires*. 1866. Reprint. Montréal: Fides, 1971.

Grandpré, Pierre de. *Histoire de la littérature française du Québec*. 4 vols. Montréal: Beauchemin, 1969.

Green, Mary Jean. "Structures of Liberation: Female Experience and Autobiographical Form in Québec." *Yale French Studies* 65 (1983): 132.

Greffard, Madeleine. "*Une Saison dans la vie d'Emmanuel:* Kaléidoscope de la réalité québécoise." *Cahiers de Sainte Marie* 1 (1966): 19–24.

Grignon, Claude-Henri. *Un Homme et son péché*. 1933. Reprint. Montréal: Stanké, 1976.

Gros-Louis, Dolores. "Pens and Needles: Daughters and Mothers in Recent Canadian Literature." *Kate Chopin Newsletter* 2.3 (1976–77): 8–15.

Guèvremont, Germaine. *Le Survenant*. 1945. Reprint. Montréal: Fides, 1984.

Guillaume, Pierre. "La Difficile affirmation d'une identité." In *Canada et Canadiens*, ed. Pierre Guillaume, Jean-Michel Lacroix, and Pierre Spriet, 11–59. Bordeaux: Presses Universitaires de Bordeaux, 1984.

Harvey, Jean-Charles. *Les Demi-civilisés*. 1934. Reprint. Montréal: L'Actuelle, 1970.

Hébert, Anne. *Le Premier jardin*. Paris: Seuil, 1988.

———. *Le Torrent*. 1965. Reprint. Montréal: Hurtubise HMH, 1976.

Hébert, Pierre. "Le Roman québécois depuis 1975: Quelques aspects saillants." *The French Review* 51.6 (1988): 899–909.

Hémon, Louis. *Maria Chapdelaine.* 1914. Reprint. Paris: Livre de Demain, 1931.

Jean de l'Imaculée, s.g.c., Soeur. "Angéline de Montbrun." In *Le Roman canadien-français,* ed. Paul Wyczynski, 105–22. Montréal: Fides, 1971.

Laberg, Albert. *La Scouine.* 1918. Reprint. Montréal: L'Actuelle, 1972.

Lacombe, Patrice. *La Terre paternelle.* 1846. Reprint. Montréal: Fides, 1981.

Lacroix, Jean-Michel. "Diversité ethnique et unité nationale au Canada." In *Canada et Canadiens,* ed. Pierre Guillaume, Jean-Michel Lacroix, and Pierre Spriet, 187–234. Bordeaux: Presses Universitaires de Bordeaux, 1984.

LaPierre, Laurier L., ed. *Québec: Hier et aujourd'hui.* Toronto: Macmillan, 1967.

Laurence, Margaret. *A Bird in the House.* Toronto: McClelland and Stewart, 1970.

Lauzière, Arsène. "Les Débuts du roman: 1830–1860," and "Le Roman: 1860–1900." In *Histoire de la littérature française du Québec,* ed. Pierre de Grandpré, 4 vols. Montréal: Beauchemin, 1971.

Leduc-Park, Renée. *Réjean Ducharme: Nietzche et Dionysos.* Québec: Presses de l'Université Laval, 1982.

Léger, Jean-Marc. "L'Incertitude d'un Québec mélancolique." In *Histoire des idées au Québec,* ed. Georges Vincenthier. Montréal: VLB Editeur, 1983.

Lemieux, Denise. *Une Culture de la nostalgie.* Montréal: Boréal Express, 1984.

Lewis, Paula Gilbert. *The Literary Vision of Gabrielle Roy.* Birmingham, Ala.: Summa Publications, 1984.

L'Hérault, Pierre. *Jacques Ferron: Cartographe de l'imaginarie.* Montréal: Presses de l'Université de Montréal, 1980.

Maheux-Forcier, Louise. *L'Ile joyeuse.* Ottawa: Cercle du Livre de France, 1964.

Marcotte, Gilles. "La dialectique de l'ancien et du nouveau chez Marie-Claire Blais, Jacques Ferron et Réjean Ducharme," *Voix et images* 6.1 (1980): 63–73.

———. "Marie-Claire Blais: 'Je veux aller le plus loin possible.'" *Voix et images* 8.2 (1983): 191–209.

Martin, Claire. *Dans un gant de fer.* Ottawa: Cercle du Livre de France, 1965.

Martinello, Margaret Pappert. "Self-Portraits: Autobiographical Writing in Canada." Ph.D. diss., York University, 1980.

Massé, Sylvain. "Le Déclin de l'Empire démographique Québécois." *Québec Studies* 8 (1989): 111–18.

Maynard, Fredelle Bruser. *Raisins and Almonds.* Toronto: Doubleday, 1972.

Mitchell, W. O. *Who Has Seen the Wind.* Toronto: Macmillan, 1947.

Munro, Alice. *Lives of Girls and Women.* New York: McGraw-Hill, 1971.

Nadeau, Vincent. *Marie-Claire Blais: Le Noir et le tendre*. Montréal: Presses de l'Université de Montréal, 1974.

Piccione, M. L. "Regards sur la littérature Québécoise." In *Canada et Canadiens*, ed. Pierre Guillaume, Jean-Michael Lacroix and Pierre Spriet. 243–85. Bordeaux: Presses Universitaires de Bordeaux, 1984.

Porter, John. *The Vertical Mosaic*. Toronto: University of Toronto Press, 1967.

Poulin, Jacques. *Jimmy*. Montréal: Editions du Jour, 1969.

Ricou, Laurie. *Everyday Magic: Child Languages in Canadian Literature*. Vancouver: University of British Columbia Press, 1987.

Ringuet. *Trente arpents*. Paris: Flammarion, 1938.

Roquebrune, Robert de. *Testament de mon enfance*. 1958. Reprint. Montréal: Fides, 1979.

Roy, Gabrielle. "Mon héritage du Manitoba." *Mosaic* 3.3 (1970): 69–79.

———. *Rue Deschambault*. 1955. Montréal: Stanké, 1980.

Roy-Hewitson, Louise. "Le Thème de l'enfance dans la poésie québécoise contemporaine." *Canadian Children's Literature* 18–19 (1980): 35–45.

Rudel-Tessier, Joseph. *Roquelune*. Montréal: Boréal Express, 1983.

Sainte-Marie-Eleuthère, c.n.d., Soeur. "Mythes et symboles de la mère dans le roman canadien-français." In *Le Roman canadien français*, ed. Paul Wyzcynski, 197–205. Montréal: Fides, 1971.

St. Pierre, Louise D. "Les Enfants et les adolescents dans l'oeuvre de Marie-Claire Blais." Ph.D. diss., University of Alberta, 1969.

Sarkar, Eileen. "The Uncertain Countries of Jacques Ferron and Mordecai Richler." *Canadian Fiction Magazine* 13 (1974): 98–107.

Sarkonak, Ralph. Preface. *Yale French Studies* 65 (1983): iii–vi.

Shek, Ben-Zion. *Social Realism in the French Canadian Novel*. Montréal: Harvest House, 1977.

Smart, Patricia. "My Father's House: Exploring Patriarchal Culture." *Canadian Forum*, December 1987.

Sutherland, Ronald. *Second Image: Comparative Studies in Québec Canadian Literature*. Don Mills, Ontario: New Press, 1971.

Thomas, Audrey. *Songs My Mother Taught Me*. Vancouver: Talonbooks, 1973.

Tougas, Gérard. *History of French-Canadian Literture*, trans. Alta Lind Cook. Westport, Conn.: Greenwood Press, 1976.

Vanasse, André. "Analyse de textes de Réjean Ducharme et Victor-Lévy Beaulieu: Les Mots et les choses." *Voix et Images* 3.2 (1977): 23.

Vallières, Pierre. *Nègres blancs d'Amérique* Ottawa: Parti Pris, 1967.

Warwick, Jack. *L'Appel du nord dans la littérature canadienne-française*. Montréal: Hurtubise HMH, 1972.

Waelti-Walters, Jennifer. "Guilt: The Prison of This World." *Canadian Literature* 88 (1981): 47–51.

Wyczynski, Paul. "Témoignages des romanciers canadiens-français," in *Le Roman canadien-français*. Montréal: Fides, 1971.

Index

85